Lawrence & Wishart L

144a OLD SOUTH LAMBETH ROAD, LONL

☎ 0171-820 9281 Fax 0171-587 0469

Date as postmark

Dear author,

Thank you for sending in a proposal to us. I am sorry to say that
we are not able to include your work in our programme.

We are small publisher with limited resources and quite a lot of
titles piled up for future publication. And I'm afraid we simply
are not able to include you. Nor do we have the resources to go
into individual reasons for not proceeding with submitted
material or to enter into individual correspondence. However, I
can assure you that we look at every piece of work that comes in
and take up any suggestion that seems appropriate to our list.

I am returning the material you sent us and wish you luck with
finding another publisher.

Yours sincerely,

Sally Davison
Director

● Regd. Office, 144a Old South Lambeth Road, London SW8 1XX
● Co. Regn. No. 310922 (London), VAT No. 233 1700 09

original returned & destroyed S.A.G.   29A

P.F.52673/C.3.   18th October, 1941.

Dear

               Miss Nancy WHITTAKER.

               Thank you for your letter of the 8th
October on this case.

               Our records of this woman show that she is
a Communist and a close friend of members of the
Communist Party.   Her flat at 36, Clare Court, Judd
Street, W.C.1. is used as a meeting place for Holborn
extremists, and is frequented by several persons of
whom we have adverse records.   Co-habiting with her
is an individual who is known as an extremely active
member of the Communist Party and a close friend of
Harry Pollitt.

               Had this woman not been appointed in the
interim, we certainly would have advised, on the
records in our possession, against her acceptance.
In the circumstances we would raise no objection
to her continued employment provided that she
does not have access to very confidential or
secret information.

                         Yours sincerely,

                         H.W.H. Sams.

D.B.Woodburn, Esq.,
    Ministry of Information,
        Malet Street,
            London W.C.1.
2

Twenty–Nine Thousand Nights

A Communist Life
Nan Berger

A project by Ruth Ewan
Book Works

4

LONDON AIRPORT

COPY

METROPOLITAN POLICE (Special Branch)

SPECIAL REPORT

ENCL

TO ..... B.I.A. Direct

REF ..... PF 52673

112a

2nd day of September 1949

Nancie BERGER, British, subject of Special Branch Port Suspect Book, left this airport for Brussels at 9.30 a.m. this day, en route for Warsaw.

She was accompanied by her two small children, both girls, and stated that she would remain in Warsaw for a few months.

As BERGER had passed through Customs before presenting herself at the Immigration barrier no special search was arranged. The examining officer afterwards stated that he noted nothing of interest to Special Branch during his clearance of her baggage.

R. H. Grinval

Constable

Submitted

Sergeant

Williamson

CHIEF SUPERINTENDENT

9.9.49

Foreword
Vicki Berger

I'M DELIGHTED THAT Ruth Ewan came across my mother's archive and found her unpublished autobiography an interesting basis for this book. It had been an earlier pleasure that the Women's Library accepted Nan's papers into their archives, which are now to be found at LSE. My thanks go to Book Works which saw the potential of Ruth's project. It has been rewarding working with them, namely Jane Rolo and Gavin Everall. With their enthusiasm, together with Nicole Bachmann's diligent photographs of images of Nan and the work of designers Osasto, the previously unpublished story of a woman committed to many worthwhile causes of the twentieth century has been brought to life.

CHILDREN'S RIGHTS

**DE-SCHOOLING:
DUANE ON
ILLICH**

**SEX BOOKS
FOR KIDS**

"You never know what waters hold until you fish in them."

— Nan Berger writing to Tony Smythe, General Secretary of the National Council for Civil Liberties 1967

RUTH EWAN   I first came across your mother's work on a visit to the Liberty (formerly the National Council for Civil Liberties) Archive at Hull City Archives. Liberty's Archive contains 153 linear metres of material and I somehow quickly honed in on Nan's name, firstly as one of the few women's names that kept reappearing, and then her range of interests seemed distinctly female – the rights of children and young people, women's rights, the politics of food, alternative education… Where do you think this interest in emancipatory politics began?

VICKI BERGER   It would seem that Nan's observations of the treatment of the workforce at her father's works showed her that she wasn't living in a fair world. Her father had some contradictory ideas about conspicuous consumption. While he flaunted his smart cars, expensive clothes, and showy food, he concealed his wealth from his workers. When his children visited the works, they covered their posh clothes with overalls, ostensibly to protect them. In fact it was to conceal them from envious eyes of the underpaid staff. She was aware of unemployment at the age of four and soon realised that she was living a luxurious life.

THE TIMES EDUCATIONAL
SUPPLEMENT   ISSUE
DATED   22 OCT 1971
PRINTING HOUSE SQUARE,
LONDON, E.C.4

Children get their voice

Children's Rights, a magazine which which will be a national information pool, a children's rights advisory service and an open forum for dialogue across the generation gap is to start publishing next month.

The magazine, says the editor Mr Julian Hall, who edited a book published earlier in the year also called *Children's Rights,* will be a "central point for a decentralized movement". The movement, he said had grown up spontaneously all over the country.

"It will be a clearing house for ideas and a place to exchange experiences and difficulties. We will give real help to those who ask for it." The magazine aims to do this through the help of an editorial board which includes A. S. Neill, headmaster of Summerhill School, Michael Duane, former headmaster of Risinghill School. Islington. Leila Berg, the author and educationist, and Nan Berger, journalist and education writer.

The magazine will tell readers where to find projects, campaigns, free schools and groups working with children. In return it wants everyone involved in any kind of work in this field to write to the magazine and tell people about it.

"There is no question of there being an organization, leadership or structure—it will be a voice for people working for and with children", said Mr Hall.

Finding herself bored by Southport's superficial social scene in which she was expected to participate, acutely aware of how inadequate her education had been, she started spending a lot of time in the local library. Although her brother was younger, he became politicised earlier. Nan attributes this to his superior education, being male. She started to buy the *Manchester Guardian* to keep herself informed, as the newspaper she found at home was the right wing *Daily Mail.* She identifies the fixed trial of those Communists accused of starting the Reichstag fire in 1933 as her real political awakening.

RE From Liberty's Archive I was led to the Women's Library at the London School of Economics which holds three boxes of material on Nan, including her previously unpublished autobiography which you donated to the Library. Why did you feel it was important to place this material in the public realm?

VB I answer this from a purely personal point of view. I am inclined to sort and organise papers.

12

I went through the papers, manuscripts, diaries, press cuttings, rejection slips, scrapbooks, etc. I threw away the many slips from publishers rejecting various novels and plays. Rightly or wrongly, I threw away these works of fiction which I considered mediocre. I thought what I kept gave an interesting narrative of a woman's life in an exciting and changing era. I was very pleased that Nan's archive found a place in the public realm, brilliantly catalogued by The Women's Library.

RE Early on during the nineteen thirties and forties in particular she is writing for many different journals and magazines under a series of pseudonyms. Do you know why?

VB Probably two reasons – the most significant was that using her maiden name, Nancie Whittaker, or her married name, Nan Berger, could have identified her as a member of the Communist Party. This would have had a detrimental effect on my father's career. Like Nan, at this time I think he was a 'withdrawn' member. Roland's main career, started in the nineteen fifties, was to be the director of the British Council for the Promotion of International Trade. Earlier he had worked for the London County Council Housing department, and the United Nations.

The number of pseudonyms may reflect different personas she wanted to assume.

RE Ideas of distribution, fairness and equality seem key to her thinking, and this is perhaps demonstrated in her work for the Ministry of Fuel and Power for which she was awarded an OBE in 1948. Do you think she felt conflicted at all, accepting this as a Communist?

VB She obviously felt some conflict but rationalised her decision to accept the OBE on the grounds that as she had no educational qualifications whatsoever, she would make good use of her honour. She told me years later that it was very useful to have some letters after her name. She was criticised for accepting it.

She was not making any feminist point at this time. During the WW2 period and just after there were many women doing jobs previously only done by men. However, earlier she had stressed her father's negative attitude to girls being educated properly and women working outside the home.

RE Her skill seems to have been in data research, statistics and the practical application of her findings.

VB Nan was a natural facilitator and organiser. She found useful things to do, like weeding the garden or moving piles of logs, for any of my teenage generation who were hanging around our house doing nothing. Her younger brother, Peter Whittaker, was a bright young man, student at LSE, fighter in the International Brigade in Spain and prisoner of Franco, soldier in the British Army in India in WW2. Post war, he had a 'collar and tie' job as a researcher and negotiator in the white-collar union, the Institute of Professional Civil Servants. It would seem that his left wing views were known but accepted/ignored until the defection of Burgess and Maclean to the Soviet Union in 1951. Following this he underwent a breakdown, leaving his employment on grounds of ill health and bringing his professional career to a premature end.

Observing her much loved brother, a bright man, now depressed, doing nothing, Nan initiated the setting up of Data-Research, a two person 'business', to give Peter a job, using his research expertise and Nan's experience in publishing. They took on one-off research projects and developed a monthly publication called *Middle East Economic Digest*. The deadline for this was too much for Peter and the business was abandoned. Sometime later, another 'make work project' was DataPrint, a typesetting business as the use of metal type was being replaced, before word processors and computers took over. A lot of their work came from the left: Topic Records, Child Poverty Action Group, etc.

In later years, after a mental breakdown, she attended sessions at a local centre for older people with psychiatric problems. She recovered well, with improved medication. She thrived on the activity at the centre and the focus it gave her. Visiting Nan one day at that time, I found her sorting through a pile of cassettes of recorded jazz. 'What are these for?' I asked. 'For my group,' she replied. Despite being well again, she had resisted discharge from the centre so was offered a place running a therapy group, her skills as an organiser (and a good listener) having been recognised by the staff. It was good for her and, I hope, for her group.

RE From the MI5 files released posthumously we can see both her personal and political life were closely monitored from 1936, following her involvement in the Anti-Fascist movement, and we can now see she was dismissed from the Bank of England because of her political beliefs. Do you think she had a sense she was being monitored?

VB I doubt that she had any idea that she and her siblings were being monitored by the police for their political activities in Southport, despite being rather conspicuous, I imagine. I trust she didn't drive her father's

The rights of the child

No one knows what to do with children. This is a society which pampers and ill-treats them, subsidises their baby-food and tolerates child poverty, glorifies their future and underinvests in their education, looks for originality and genius and yet tries to enforce convention upon each succeeding generation, in dress, in morals, and in political and religious attitudes.

The ambivalence of society towards the child is the theme of *The Rights of Children and Young Persons*, a study promoted by the National Council of Civil Liberties. All the incidents of childhood are examined in terms of rights bestowed and rights denied, and the analysis is illuminating.

Yet mere statement of a "right" conveys little. The language of "rights" is a form of political shorthand which presupposes, and sometimes deliberately avoids, the formulating of underlying principles. For the argument to be fully understood, those principles must be explored.

Philosophically, the state of the child is a compound of three factors. First, society's general ideas about the nature of man and his conduct: original sin, heredity, the primacy of mind, and his perfectability. Secondly, conventions of parenthood, often crude and unsympathetic with man as parent reproducing uncritically in his treatment of children the treatment he received as a child: it is a body of general ideas which is highly resistant to change. Thirdly, the political philosophy of the child, or perhaps more accurately, the principles which guide government, central and local, in its dealings with children and their affairs. The rise in the school leaving age, the cuts in free school milk, and even the day-to-day administration of the schools, the welfare services, and the grant systems—all reveal, and have implications for, that governmental philosophy.

Of these, it is the philosophy of government which deserves the most attention. Which is not to say it is the most important: the other factors determine the child's fate in the long term, and it is their interplay which is responsible for the prevailing ambivalence. But it is by the action of government that change will primarily be effected.

The central question of any governmental philosophy is this: to what extent is the child to be acknowledged as having its own rights and interests independently of its parents, with a claim to their recognition and enforcement by the community?

It is a provocative question. For instance, it forces to the surface an ambiguity which is endemic to government action: the promotion of child welfare and education may be founded either on a Bismarckian interest in the economic and military resources of the nation or on a recognition, as a matter of political philosophy, of the individual's right to the full development of his physical and mental capacity. Both approaches often produce the same result, in terms of the allocation of resources; but their implications for society, and for the style and atmosphere of education, are very different.

The question also brings out the difference between the philosophy of a static society, in which the child is subsumed uncritically to the status of its parents, and a society in which an attempt is made to diminish the importance of family ties, along the lines of the traditional socialist concern with "reshuffling the cards" in each generation.

The question also demands a review of present trends. Since the last war there has developed a stronger link than ever before between governmental institutions and the child, independently of the parent. This is particularly so in its early years, with the promotion of child health. School attendance is enforced between five and 15 and the tendency is for education authorities and the teaching profession, despite PTAS, to develop a philosophy of education which establishes a direct link with the child, by-passing the parents. And there is much more public supervision of children in their own homes.

It is true that both Plowden and current child care theory go out of their way to stress the importance of the parent, but they only do so because the mainstream is flowing the other way. School leaving at 16 and more nursery schooling would reinforce the trend. So would the abolition of parental means tests for student grants.

Both the declining role of the parent and the increasing role of the state suggest that still greater recognition should be given to the child and his interests. The emphasis of child psychology on parental affection and a full parent-child relationship does not contradict this. Indeed, it is rooted in the belief that children should be treated as individuals with their own rights. The state and the law should reinforce this notion.

---

smart cars to Party meetings. (The Chief Constable of Southport wrote to Vernon Kell at MI5 on the matter.)

As politically active teenagers, my sister and I were advised not to talk about politics on the phone, as my parents rightly assumed that the phone was tapped. She would frequently visit the CPGB HQ in Covent Garden, leaving me sitting outside in the car. She must have assumed that the car registration number was known to the authorities.

It was relatively recently, in 2009, that my attention was drawn to Christopher Andrew's *The Defence of the Realm, The Authorised History of MI5*. He wrote that a lodger in our house was a planted MI5 agent, who facilitated a raid on the house while we were away. They removed some thousands of documents, which they copied and returned. Apparently these were details of the membership of the CPGB being stored 'in a safe place'. Both my parents were dead by the time this came to light so I was unable to ask them if they knew about these MI5 activities. This subsequently led me to the National Archives at Kew, where I have read MI5 files of surveillance of both my parents.

RE The autobiography focuses on her own upbringing, the formation of her early political identity and her travels to the USA, South Africa, and China. Was it written mainly from travel journals?

VB Yes, the only one I still have is from our year in Poland.

RE She misses out much of her personal research work, books, and her later family life: her marriage to Roland, for example – we only first come to him late on in the book.

VB She mentions Roland (aka Lucky) early on, soon after joining the CP in Holborn. He was involved in left wing Agit Prop Theatre. He features in the chapter on our year in Poland in 1949.

It amuses me to recall my mother, an independent thinking feminist, on the eve of my father's return from his many journeys abroad, rushing around to secure a loaf of Mother's Pride or some similar low grade white sliced bread for my gourmet father's breakfast. (This was before convenience stores stayed open late.)

Ironically, Nan's independence and her ability to leave my father when she was in her sixties was facilitated by her ownership of the family house, bought with money from her father. So, although my Grandfather

Schofield would have liked to see his daughters as dutiful wives and mothers, his money gave them an independence and freedom unusual for women of their generation.

RE Her book *Women Fancy or Free?* published in 1962 predates what is thought of as second-wave feminism, with much of the research and development of this book happening in the 1950s.

VB *Woman, Fancy or Free?* is a strange book and I don't recall that it made any impact. It barely mentions sex and was published by Mills and Boon. (Virago didn't start until 1973.) It was written from an economic viewpoint. Simone de Beauvoir's *The Second Sex* was published in 1949. Nan and her co-author and lifelong friend, Joan Maizels, wrote to de Beauvoir in Paris and secured an invitation from her to lunch. They arrived in Paris (no Eurostar then) to discover that they had been stood up by de Beauvoir. She apologised and a subsequent meeting was arranged.

RE Also her research into the social purpose of school meals and discussions around children's rights in the early 1970s seem truly pioneering – would you agree?

VB Yes, and it should be seen in the context of events like the *Oz* trial (1971), Michael Duane and Risinghill School, etc. Her interest in school meals developed, I imagine, from her involvement with NASMO (National Association of School Meals Organisers) when she was editor of a magazine dealing with catering management in the public sector. She was interviewed by Derek Cooper for Radio 4's *The Food Programme*.

RE Did Nan keep her left wing views in later life?

VB The election of 1997 was the last Nan witnessed. I remember saying 'Anything has to be better than the Tories,' to which she replied 'I'm not sure you're right about that.' When Blair won the election a friend brought her a red plant in celebration. Her reaction to that was 'Not sure you've got the right colour for this Labour government.'

Twenty–Nine Thousand Nights

A Communist Life
Nan Berger

CHILDREN'S RIGHTS

15P

Hung up from birth?

I
Birth in the Night

MAY, 1937.

"I said I was sorry, but I had another engagement."

The Other Side of the KITCHEN DOOR

by N. WHITTAKER

SO now we domestic servants are to be called " Domesticians " in order to raise our status. What difference will it make ? A long time ago Shakespeare said " What's in a name ? That which we call a rose, by any other name would smell as sweet."

You can change the name of an occupation once in every month, but if the system is rotten it won't make any difference.

I have been a maid for twelve months. I used to work in a factory, but when things got slack they laid me off and there was no other work, so I went to an agency and they offered me a job at fifteen shillings a week, and " all found." When I had taken the job they told me I owed them my first week's wages as a fee.

I got to the place in time to lay the table and help the cooks with the vegetables for dinner. The mistress seemed pleasant but not very definite with her orders. For instance, she never told me she wanted the vegetables served from the side and then grumbled when I handed them round. She was constantly changing her mind. First it would be dinner at seven, then half-past and within half an hour she would be in the kitchen again changing back to seven.

We arranged that I should have every other Saturday evening and every Wednesday from three o'clock off. I said it was not much, but my mistress promised to allow me out sometimes after dinner was cleared.

For the first two months everything was fine. No breakages to pay for and three times she popped into the kitchen about half-past eight and said I could go out. It was a relief to get a breath of fresh air after the hot fire in the kitchen, especially on Mondays when the clothes were drying in the kitchen. Then one Wednesday she came into the kitchen about 11.30 a.m. and asked me to stay in as she had friends coming. I said I was sorry, but I had an engagement and she could hardly expect me to give up my only free time.

" But think of all those extra evenings you have had," she said.

" But you never tell me I can go out until it is too late for anything but a walk," I replied. " That is not really free time. It's too uncertain."

She was very annoyed and the next week I got the sack. Not suitable !

When I had taken a train to my next job (at twelve shillings a week this time) paid my insurance, the agency and sent my five shillings a week home, I had £3 2s. 6d. left for nine weeks work. Seven shillings a week to spend on my clothes, outings and savings stamps !

I've heard mistresses say that they change faults when they change maids. I certainly changed for the worst. I am on my feet from six thirty in the morning until ten at night. I get one half-day and an occasional Sunday afternoon. No question of a few hours in the evening here. When I complain about the long hours the mistress says : " But you don't have a thing to do between lunch and dinner."

That is nearly true, but I can't go out or settle to anything because of the telephone and bells which are always ringing. It isn't free time at all. Just monotonous inactivity. I'd be better fully occupied.

Funny how ignorant some mistresses are. When I said that twelve bob a week did not give you much chance to save for when you were out of work my mistress said : " My husband pays taxes so you can draw the dole." It took me a long time to convince her that domestic servants can't draw dole.

I wish I could go back to the factory. The work there was hard and the wages poor, but you could call your life your own after six o'clock. Decent wages and proper living conditions would do a lot to improve matters in this " profession," but its the long hours and loneliness that are the real bother. No one ought to be shut up in a house, often with nobody to talk to, for hours at a time like we are. I've never had a place where you could have your man friends to tea, but often your girl friends can come. That is all very well, but what if she is in the same position as you are ? She doesn't want to spend her afternoon off cooped up in someone else's kitchen.

I have a loud speaker in the kitchen, but the wireless is only on when the family are in. I wouldn't care if it were never on as long as I had more free time.

I've worked ninety-six hours this week for twelve shillings less insurance. I know dailies are badly paid, but if I drew tenpence an hour like the daily does on Tuesdays I would have earned four pounds this week !

What is to be done ? Perhaps it looks a hopeless problem, but I think if there were more organisation and planning ahead done by the mistress our hours could be very much shortened. If there were more thought for our personal happiness and less treatment like machines our jobs would be more bearable. If we were entrusted with the food buying, and the planning of meals our life would be more interesting. But above all more free time that really is free time and not just wasted inactivity.

I WAS BORN IN the night. I was nearly born in the restaurant at the Midland Hotel, Manchester, a favourite haunt of my parents, but by a bit of good management my mother was transported home in my father's eggshell blue open Napier with brass headlamps, and I was born in time for my mother to make a recovery before breakfast time and eat some bacon and eggs at half past eight. So with dinner at the Midland the night before, my mother did not miss any meals on my account. I retained a special relationship with the Midland Hotel, cajoling various boyfriends who could not really afford it to take me there for dinner or to a *thé dansant*. The relationship lasted until 1971 when it came to an abrupt end. As the climax to a nostalgic tour of the northern places I had known as a child, my younger daughter, her male escort and myself decided to live it up on our last night with a night's stay and dinner at the Midland. We booked dinner by phone from the hotel bedroom. When we presented ourselves my daughter and myself were dressed in our best trousers and shirts, which were clean and tidy if not entirely appropriate, and our male escort was dressed in his best suit with a polo neck sweater, fashionable at the time. We were refused entry because he was not wearing a tie. I never felt the same again about the Midland.

So that accounts for two of the nights in my life. What happened on the other 28,998?

Night can be regarded as either the end of the day or a beginning. Perhaps because of the circumstances of my birth I have always looked upon nights as a beginning: a prelude, an introduction to more vigorous activity. Nights are not remembered for their romance – whatever romance there has been in my life has not been at night – but rather for their clarity, their excitement, their creative possibilities.

Night becomes life – days are for practical things. Night is for thinking, for dreaming.

Sleep can be very productive. Problems formulated in semi-consciousness can be solved in dream state. More importantly, the past can be resurrected. Thinking about a past event can produce a dream elaborating the sequence. Morning is the time for sorting out the reality from the fantasy.

I have largely reconstructed the past and pieced together the jigsaw of my life. The nights, sometimes half sleepless in old age, have become a life, a life to be looked forward to as physical activities become less possible. I anticipate that as daily routine tasks become more difficult and life becomes chair-sitting and bed-lying, living a life in dreams will become really important in keeping a mind alive and interested in still being a life. For the moment the night and the dream are a tool, like a typewriter, recording a life spanning two world wars and an almost complete change of attitudes and concepts.

Was it a dream that my father, totally drunk, arrived on his own doorstep, armed with bunches of dead flowers, at least twice a week? I never actually saw it but I have been told about it so many times that I now believe it. He was almost a Jekyll and Hyde figure. Everyone except his own family thought he was a most charming, considerate man. To his wife he was an irresponsible, extravagant husband who drank too much and kept her short of money; to his children a stern, distant figure who made their mother cry. The truth was somewhere in between. My mother cried because she had married the wrong man and never ceased to let my father know it. She had chosen my father because he had money and the man she really loved was a penniless bank clerk with no prospects. She herself had extravagant ideas, she loved clothes, and she hated living in a two-up and two-down where her children played in a back alley. She resented the money which was spent on the Napier, which was the envy of the neighbourhood and rarely used except to take the family, my grandfather and my father's younger brother, to Blackpool for tea at the Imperial Hotel.

Although she deplored the amount of money lavished on the car she polished the brass headlamps while other women in the street scrubbed and whitened their front steps and the step at their front gates. Ours remained un-whitened and stuck out like a snobbish gesture against wasted time, though our backyard was always the best swept and our back garden, separated from the yard and house by an alleyway in which we played, was always the best kept. It was in this alleyway that Peter, my younger brother, got a stone struck in his throat. My mother panicked and started screaming. A neighbour heard the screams, saw the child gagging on the stone, picked him up by the heels and threw him over her shoulder. At the third throw, he coughed up the stone. It was the neatest piece of life saving I have ever seen.

We were too young to drive the Napier but later, when it was changed for a Bentley, we learned to drive in that. Learning to drive was also part of learning to live. It was a serious business, a necessary skill for boys and girls alike. At sixteen, lessons started in the driveway of our house in the 1926 Bentley with a non-synchromesh gate gearbox and brakes on the back wheels only. To change gear required a well-timed double de-clutch. If you missed it you had to stop and start again. Our tutor was one of Bentley's own mechanics called Jim who patiently coached us in the art of proper driving. If we hit something his expression never changed. When, in 1940, I joined the war ambulance service his teaching stood me in good stead. Of all the people at the station only three could drive the converted Albion vans. The other two who could manage these horrors were lorry drivers. We called the vans banana ambulances because they were loaned by Fyffes, the banana importers, and still had the yellow signs painted on the sides depicting a bunch of bananas. To this day, I double de-clutch on any car I drive. Most people under seventy don't know what it means.

One of the treats we had as children was visiting my father's works in the Hollinwood area of Oldham. He dealt in cotton waste, buying gunny (the bale coverings of imported cotton), picking off the cotton, mending the gunny, and baling it for shipment back to the United States. The sale of the cotton waste made some money but it was the baled gunny which made the biggest profits, the epitome of the phrase 'where there's muck there's money'. He also bought the rags used in the engineering trade, squeezed the oil from them and resold the dry rags, as well as the oil.

When we visited the works there was always a great palaver about wearing white cotton coats. We put them on in his office before we went into the warehouse where the work was done. My father explained that the coats would protect us from the flying dust. Later we found out from my father's younger brother who was employed in the firm that it was nothing to do with dust. It was so that the workers would not see what good clothes we wore and become discontented because they could not buy such clothes for their own children. Profits in those days were something you kept secret – or so my father thought.

For the same reason my father's office was never given any sort of refurbishment. The paint flaked off the walls and the furniture was the same he had purchased when he founded the firm in 1898 when he was eighteen years old, six years after he left school. There were two rooms in the office: one for my grandfather – whose name was Handel, which was the name etched into the plate glass window that overlooked the yard where the horse lorries were loaded – and my father; and one for my uncle and the typist. There was also a lavatory and a kitchen which were almost one room. No one thought it at all extraordinary to have food prepared next door to the lavatory, though in fact the three men never used the kitchen for their lunch. Every day steaks were cooked over the open fire in my father's office. Handel walked down the road to the butcher's shop which was owned by his cousin Jasper who kept aside the best pieces of rump for him. Only three steaks were bought. The typist Miss Johnson – I never knew her first name although she was with the firm until long after my father died – brought her own sandwiches and ate them at her desk. The workers stayed on the premises for their dinner, paying the woman in charge of cleaning the boiler house a penny a week to mash their tea in blue cans which they brought with them daily, complete with sugar and milk already mixed up, ready for the boiling water.

The scruffiness and poor image of my father's office and works was in strong contrast to the luxury in which he lived. No fear here that his workers would see his affluence. It was too far away. And so the works' class structure was maintained, and it remained so until my father's death in 1942.

By the time I was four years old I knew what unemployment was. In the neighbourhood around our house in New Moston, near Oldham, one could see groups of men squatting on their heels at street corners. My father called them wasters but Lizzie, the housekeeper at Raven's Leach, my Grandfather Crossley's home, told me there was no work for them. The date was 1918. The First World War was nearly over; many of them never worked again. Lizzie's husband was a postman and she was terrified he would lose his job and persuaded him to buy some pigs and keep them in the unused sty at Raven's Leach, quite near to home but no one seemed to mind the smell. By the time their first child was born – called Nancie after me – his pigs were making more money than his regular job so he moved them elsewhere and had another child.

The two-up two-down in New Moston where I was born was changed for a four-bedroomed detached house in Southport when I was four. Southport was a seaside town on the Ribble Estuary where the sea rarely got nearer to the shore than a mile and which served, among other things, as a dormitory for prosperous businessmen who worked in nearby Manchester and Liverpool. The house was a gigantic step up but it did not satisfy my father for long. He made a slightly shady deal with a drunken horse dealer for a house in a better part of the town and saddled my mother with a solidly built, Victorian atrocity with three 'reception' rooms, a cloakroom far larger than today's average bedroom, huge kitchens, a scullery, a butler's pantry, ten bedrooms, a massive garden and stabling for four horses. There were also large cellars, one for food with a stone topped table about ten-feet square, a wash cellar, a storage cellar, a coal cellar, and a wine cellar. Every evening of his affluent life my father took an empty decanter down to the wine cellar and filled it with whisky from a barrel which came straight from a distillery in Scotland. He started drinking the whisky when he came home at five o'clock and by ten it was finished. Sometimes he would traipse down to the cellar for a refill. Yet I saw him incapable on only one occasion.

Drink in our house was part of a way of life. My father taught himself about wines and I cannot recall seeing non-vintage bottles on our table. Alcohol was never locked up. We could take a drink when we wanted even when we were about twelve. But if ever we drank too much, more than we could hold, there were serious consequences and lectures about self-discipline. It was all part of learning to live.

The one drink you were permitted to get slightly drunk on was champagne. It came in wooden cases and was vintage Cliquot. I remember, in later years, hearing my father say that Cliquot '47 was the best drink in the world. By this time I had realised that not all the world drank champagne and regarded a bottle of almost any kind of champagne as a great treat.

How to eat oysters was also part of learning to live, and it was done on a grand scale. The fishmonger would be summoned on a Sunday morning to bring oysters and his opening gear. He used the scullery table as his work bench and we ate the oysters in the kitchen. A dozen each was about the ration. Eating oysters was not particularly unusual. You could then eat a plateful at the market stall for a reasonable price. What was unusual was having the fishmonger come to the house. Later in life I realised that this sort of thing was all part of the struggle for conspicuous wealth. Unable to compete academically or intellectually my father tried to gain recognition through his wealth but in a slightly eccentric way.

Most of the affluence we displayed did not affect me. I just took it in my stride and thought it normal procedure but the part attached to my clothes caused me a lot of embarrassment. My mother was constantly buying me clothes she thought suitable, which were far better and flashier than any my friends or school mates had. One needed a special sort of self-confidence to carry off such clothes. She had it and to a lesser degree so did my elder sister but I did not, and it caused me a lot of pain to have to wear clothes that made people turn around in the street.

Yet, in spite of the champagne and the foie gras, our household was in many ways frugal. To waste anything, particularly food, was considered a crime. All household expenditure was carefully scrutinised and we had less pocket money than most of our friends. If, on occasions, we were given extra money to go on a trip to see friends, it had to be accounted for down to the last penny. I remember the routine well. You wrote what you had spent item by item, on paper and handed it to my father, along with the change. It would remain on the table by his chair until bedtime. If he were in a good mood he gave you the change as he kissed you goodnight. I sometimes longed for a few quid for which I did not have to account and which I could spend on a frivolity. I had to wait until I was sixteen to get it. It came in the form of a dress allowance and was paid in cash quarterly. I could spend it how I liked but I had to be properly dressed to conform with family standards so there was not a lot for other things.

My mother's father, Abraham, lived in a large house in New Moston on the edge of what we called the 'whitestuff', a chalky piece of ground near the canal overlooking Ferranti's factory, probably the first they ever built. Behind the house were the works where my grandfather and his son Tom made Jacquard machines which were fitted to weaving looms to make patterns on fabrics, as on damask tablecloths. When we visited the works we were given tasks to do – mainly arranging small springs in flat trays. This earned us our tea which was invariably a fruit pie with Carnation milk prepared for us by Florrie, who was my grandfather's housekeeper and who in fact ruled the family for many years. Before I was born my grandmother did the spring placing jobs sitting at the kitchen table so that she was available to the salesmen who called for orders and the buyers who wanted the Jacquard apparatus for their looms. She was a woman anxious to improve herself and to this end she bought a child's writing book to help her with her handwriting. She copied out the trite sentences for a time and when she got fed up with them she invented some of her own. One was 'Better fart and be blamed than fill your britches and be shamed'. She was writing it when a salesman called – they didn't knock and walked straight in as the kitchen door was never closed. He asked her what she was doing and she explained. He asked to see the book and in her naive way she handed it to him. He never called again.

The main market for my grandfather's Jacquard machines was Russia. After the Revolution the demand for self-patterned fabrics was not all that buoyant and gradually the men who worked in the almost feudal conditions of the works drifted off into the large spinning mills in the area, leaving my grandfather and my uncle Tom to do what work there was left. Tom had been trained at the Daimler Motor Company in his apprentice days and one of his jobs there was to teach the coachmen of wealthy mill owners, who bought cars at the beginning of the century, to drive. At the same time, he worked in the design shop of Daimler and had a promising career there. My grandfather disliked the idea of his son becoming someone who was successful in his own right and hauled him back to the Jacquard works to try to pull the business out of decline. In a situation doomed to failure Tom devoted most of his time to racing pigeons and the rest to just sitting, which he continued until his death. My grandfather, Abraham, took to sitting too; there was nothing much else to do, and I can remember him spitting into the fire from a distance of two yards from his eternal sitting position. Every time his wife saw him doing it she delivered a lecture about culture which is how she referred to good manners. Abraham had no respect for people. He suffered them un-gladly, and when his eldest son became a drug addict, a result of his contact with ether in the hospital where he worked during the First World War, he threw him out and let him die more or less on the streets.

Raven's Leach, as my grandfather's house was called, was an open house. People came and went in the house as they did in the factory behind it. Sometimes I stayed the night in the big room overlooking the pigeon loft at the back. On one of these nights I was awakened by some shouting. I heard a voice say, 'Mr Crossley, your back door is open, and I heard my grandfather snap back 'Well shut it.' I learned in the morning that the first speaker was a policeman.

For his daughters, my grandfather had a little more regard and acquiesced to his wife's demand that they be sent to a finishing school in France. The three of them went off to learn French, embroidery, good manners, and deportment. The youngest of them, Mabel, learned none of these things as she was too busy flirting with any Frenchman with the time and inclination. My mother, Hannah (Tannie for short), learned them all plus piano playing. The third, Maggie, became ill and died at home when she was less than twenty-five from a 'broken-heart' which was probably consumption. But the spell in France did give my mother a wider view of life than that of her future husband, Schofield, my father. I doubt if he ever read anything other than detective stories and Charles Dickens and he certainly never listened to any music. The home in which his three children were brought up was entirely devoid of any kind of culture: few books, no music, no real conversation, plenty of well-being in the material sense but little love. When I started serious reading it was almost secretly in the local public library. To my father, reading by the young was a sign of laziness. His idea of what women should do centred round darning socks, caring for the house, and preparing for marriage – none of which, he claimed, needed books.

II
A Nouveau
Riche Life

END KITCHEN SLAVERY!

Domestic Workers' Union Is Vital To Hampstead

By MAURICE WHITTAKER

WHILE one person in every 57 in Stepney is a domestic servant, the ratio is one in every seven in Hampstead. What an important event the forming of a Domestic Servants' Union is for the Borough!

In 1931, there were nearly 12,000 people in service in this area, and the numbers have probably increased since, owing to the transference of boys and girls from the Distressed Areas and the pressure exerted on unemployed men and women to take up this work.

In recent months there have been two separate plans put forward for improvement of conditions The first came from the Minister of Labour, representing the "National" Government. His plan is rather like the scenery they use for making films—looks fine from the front, but when you look round the back you find you've been fooled.

He wanted to form a League of Good Mistresses who would hold badges signifying that they had agreed to minimum standards. These badges, he expected, would attract young women (and young men) into service.

Unfortunately, he didn't say what the standards were or how he intended to enforce them; and when mistresses said they would have nothing to do with the scheme because it might interfere with their "liberty," and servants said they thought the scheme was a sham, he had to drop the idea and return to the less spectacular methods of transference and bullying.

Fortunately, there is another plan for domestic workers—Trade Unionism.

THE WORKERS' PLAN

For the first time, the Trades Union Congress has taken the responsibility of forming a new Union. The National Union of Domestic Workers was launched on July 1 of this year, and already has a healthy membership. The Executive Committee has just issued a charter which includes a 96-hour fortnight, holidays with pay, and written agreements.

Post-war organisation among these workers is almost unknown, but in 1897 London and provincial domestic servants carried on a successful campaign for the inclusion of servants in the Employers' Liability Act. Meetings were held in Hyde Park and the fight was won—an answer to those who say that organisation for such workers is impossible.

The responsibility of assisting these workers certainly does not lie only with the T.U.C. and the workers themselves. They have not the traditional background of Trade Unionism to assist them, and it is the duty of every Labour organisation to help them recruit. It is especially a task for the youth organisations. Of the million and a half workers in this occupation, over one-third are less than 25 years of age, and the continual flow of young boys and girls is rapidly increasing this figure Between 1928 and 1935, 17,787 girls have been transferred into domestic service.

UNSKILLED GIRLS FORCED INTO SERVICE

For thousands of young girls, service is the only opening for which they have any chance; and, because they enter it unskilled, they have to accept a low wage and put up with long hours and filthy living conditions.

While there may be a shortage of skilled labour at the top, there is certainly no shortage of young, untrained girls, who are forced into service as soon as they are of school-leaving age, because no other occupation has vacancies for them.

The unskilled labour market is constantly fed by the reformatories, charitable institutions and orphanages, a great percentage of whose inmates are put into service, whether they like it or not.

Domestic service may look like a healthy occupation; but the long hours indoors, and the standing on ill-shod feet, play havoc with young constitutions. Girls' minds become stagnant from lack of social contact with companions of their own age, and they become listless and dissipirited. Recently one girl wrote to me:—

"Is there any need for anyone to work 16 hours a day? Is there any need for girls of 14 and 15 to slave away, when they should still be at school having a good time? Why must the youth of to-day be the wrecks of to-morrow? That is where we shall end up! Why must our health suffer as well as our body and brains? Where is the Ministry of Health? Surely they could help! Does it take an 18-year-old to tell them that our working conditions are dangerous to health?"

MINISTRY OF APATHY

The Ministry of Health recently said it had no power to do anything about a girl of 14 who was sleeping in the basement kitchen of a small guest house, accompanied by the rubbish, the cooking stove, the central-heating boiler, and two other girls.

My correspondent ended with: "Must this go on? Can't we appeal to everyone to help us? You can count on me for one. Conditions must change."

The success of the Union depends on girls like this one, who are prepared to fight for better conditions, and on everyone who realises that the domestic problem is not a personal squabble between maids and mistresses, but one which has a class basis and is the result of our social structure. There will be mistakes and misunderstandings, but improved conditions can and will be gained through organisation.

On the other hand, just as the engineers', the shop assistants' and the errand-boys' problems will not be solved until we achieve Socialism, nor will the domestics' problems be finally removed until the class relation of mistress and maid is removed.

DOMESTIC WORKERS' UNION

THE newly formed branch is energetically tackling the task of organising the domestic workers in the district—one of the most difficult occupations to handle, because domestic workers have usually only one evening off a week.

A house-to-house canvass is being arranged so that the workers may be interviewed at their place of employment, also small informal meetings are being held at the residence of the secretary, so that it will be possible for those interested to attend, no matter on which day their evening off happens to fall.

The secretary asks readers of the "Citizen" to try and think of at least one person employed in domestic work (or in the large army of "daily helps" so well known in Hampstead), and make the Union known to them.

Maybe some readers actually employ domestic help themselves, and these are asked to encourage such workers to become active, and to take their friends to the meetings.

The secretary welcomes inquiries, and will be pleased to send literature—address, Mrs. Hall, 3, Chalcot-square, N.W. 1.

ALTHOUGH WE LIVED like the liberal middle class we were really nouveau riche, without much culture but with quite a bit of show. When we entertained it was lavish. Out came the silver and the crystal and on very special occasions, such as visits by American customers, a butler would be hired to serve the drinks and wait at table. Fortunately, such occasions as this had some of the pomp knocked out of them by my father's strong sense of the ludicrous. I can remember him saying to the butler, who was handing round the vegetables in a silver entrée dish 'You are going to be quite busy tomorrow returning all this fancy stuff to the hirer.' My mother who had probably spent hours polishing the glass and rubbing up the silver did not think this was at all funny.

My father was not a cook but he knew about cooking and he loved food. He would create a great fuss if food were not cooked as he thought it should be. Every Sunday was crisis day in our house. The menu was the same summer and winter: roast wing rib of beef, roast potatoes, marrowfat peas followed by a suet apple pudding on which my father put a splash of gin for extra flavour. The beef had to be rare, the marrowfat peas soft. The whole family would be on tenterhooks while the beef was cut. If it was overcooked my father likely as not would leave the table and my mother would cry. The children just ate. We could, by the age of ten or so, carve any sort of joint so serving ourselves was no problem. As to the peas, my mother had probably got up in the middle of the night to see whether she had remembered to put them to soak and added the tablet of something which came in the packet which was probably bicarbonate of soda to keep them green. If they were hard my father grumbled but he remained at the table. The apple suet pudding was not too crucial, the cook could hardly ruin that.

The nearest we got to 'culture' was a weekly visit to the 'flicks' where we saw whatever happened to be on – always the same cinema, the same day, the same seats – or a visit to the theatre if there were a special company visiting the town, but such outings were more for the purpose of being seen than of seeing. I do not think my father ever attended a concert in his whole life.

There was something not quite genuine about the way our family lived. Our lifestyle was based almost entirely on money values. Whatever we bought or did had to be the best. My father's watchword was 'if you cannot afford the best you cannot afford anything'. Being the 'best' did not mean being top of the class at school but being better dressed than one's classmates. It did not mean a better knowledge of what was going on in the world or a greater participation in local activities but a better estimation of how to display wealth to the best advantage. It was as though we were showing off all the time, playing some kind of game, not really being part of society. It added up to a falseness, since everything we did had to be better than the next man could do, and this attitude kept us, as individuals and as a family, out of areas where we could not compete successfully. It undermined us, as children, in attempting any activity where we were not sure of success, which effectively kept us out of academic and cultural pursuits because the results were not 'conspicuous', were not of immediate value, and did little to establish the family as a money-rich unit in a competitive world.

From the time we moved from the two-up two-down in a street in a working-class area near Manchester, to a large house in the fashionable residential area of a seaside resort, I became increasingly aware of being different. Southport was an ideal place in which to be 'different' with its unbalanced mix of population – there were very few working-class people, and a high number of retired people or businessmen who travelled daily to Manchester or Liverpool. Even our holidays were 'different'. Not for us the camping holiday or a trip abroad to find out how other people lived. When we were small we rented houses in seaside resorts like Blackpool and Anglesey. Later when we went abroad it was because my father had decided that sea voyages were the thing. We boarded a P&O steamer headed for the Far East. At Marseille we got off, stayed the night, and embarked on a similar ship on its way back to Britain.

Another of our rather odd holidays was a visit to the British Empire Exhibition at Wembley. It took place in 1924 until 1925. I was ten at the time we went. As a family, we attended the exhibition grounds every day for five days and watched endless tattoos, march pasts and demonstrations of local talent. It was probably the first time I had seen any non-white people and I was fascinated. I kept leaving the family group and sneaking off to the Indian, African and West Indies pavilions to stare in wonderment. My parents were really worried. There were whispered conversations, 'she might want to marry one', which were as ludicrous as they were unlikely. Sixty odd years ago no middle-class girl (even one ten years old) thought of marriage to someone other than one of her own class and colour.

Continuing his policy of buying only the best for himself and his family my father took us to the Savoy Hotel in 1930 for a five-day visit to see the London sights. To northerners the Savoy was Mecca, and a meal in the Savoy Grill was the height of sophistication. It was the sort of high living to which we were not accustomed, and a meal in the Grill, after the theatre (probably a musical comedy – a Cochran Revue would have been about our style), was something to really brag about. When Henry Hall, then highly popular as a 'big band' leader and with whom my father had some vague contact, joined us for supper one night, we thought we were really mixing in high society.

Until I became connected many years later with the hotel and catering industry professionally I never stayed in such an up-market hotel again. In the early thirties when I was old enough to make visits to London without my parents, I chose to stay in the annex of the Park Lane Hotel in Piccadilly rather than in a smaller hotel at my price level. One could stay in the annex for seven shillings and sixpence a night with breakfast, which you had to take in your tiny room. But you could savour the big hotel glamour in the daytime by walking through the main lobby into Piccadilly itself, or by taking tea in the hotel lounge, if you could afford it. It probably cost as much as the bed and breakfast in the annex.

Later in the thirties the newly built Cumberland Hotel at Marble Arch offered bed and breakfast in a tiny (for those days) room with a bath at ten shillings and sixpence. My brother-in-law used to stay there on his frequent visits to the capital from his overseas posting after the war, and prices were not much higher. His visits were uneventful except for one occasion. He had been persuaded by a mere acquaintance to bring with him a parcel of towels which a woman, whom he did not know, would collect on his arrival. Arrive she did within minutes of his occupation of the room. She rushed in, tore open the parcel, extracted a small box and was gone before he could even speak, leaving the towels behind her. It was the last time he ever brought so-called presents to London from people he came across in his posting.

My father's riches enabled him to employ servants. We had a cook, a parlour maid, and a housemaid as well as a 'mother's help', who was really

SET US WOMEN REALLY FREE!

By Ena Kendall

REVOLUTIONARY reflections on women and their future as human beings emerge from the pages of a modest little book which has just made its appearance.

Some of the suggestions made in "Woman—Fancy or Free?" by Nan Berger and Joan Maizels (Mills and Boon Limited; 12s. 6d. net) will certainly be greeted with howls of protest by the rigid and conventional-minded, the natural blockers of progress even when it is inevitable.

Nan Berger and Joan Maizels, one a journalist and one a sociologist, both married with children, are dedicated to the thesis that women are entitled to full and satisfying lives as human beings and should not be treated as creatures born to fulfil a pre-conceived role.

They attack the illusion that girls will grow up to spend their lives looking after children who never grow up and a family which remains always dependent. The family is composed of children who in the process of their growth become increasingly self-reliant, and of mature men who, it is assumed, are already so. The assumption that women will be exclusively tied to their families for the whole of their lives is a fantasy contradicted by the facts, they say.

Wider scope

Therefore, they believe, women should not only be educated for a life of far wider scope; they should be helped actively by the State to exercise greater choice in the way they spend their time by reformed and extended social services.

They suggest for a start that a regular domestic service, controlled by public authorities and organised on rational non-profit-making lines should be available to all women who want it.

Home helps are available in an emergency, but the ordinary woman cannot call upon them. There is no organised domestic service for the working mother, the woman with a large family. Domestic help is available only to those with the money to pay for it.

A State domestic help service would mean housework done as a job by people paid for the purpose, so releasing a wife and mother from the drudgery that has hitherto always been accepted as an inevitable part of most marriages.

They also ask if there is any difference in principle between the acceptance of a school meals service and the acceptance of one which would provide meals for the whole family. "The establishment of family restaurants as a social service could provide what private enterprise as a profit-making service now offers to those who eat away from home. The preparation of food keeps a woman tied to the kitchen sink for an appreciable part of each day. Her catering service may result in the provision of as many as 1,200 cooked meals in a year."

'Humbug'

The occasional relief provided by recourse to such family restaurants would be welcomed by many women, they suggest.

Pause here for howls of protest. Critics will maintain that increased social services sap individual initiative, indulge the morally weak, break down family life—to which the authors retort, "Nonsense and humbug. Why should a subordinate, dependent, restricted life for women be made to appear in the natural law of things?"

They believe that all kinds of modifications are possible, particularly through the provision of more public services and the scientific study of each repetitive chore, to re-evaluate the way in which many women spend their lives. Woman's role, they point out, is still that of a private domestic servant to her husband and family. Women are still involved in cleaning up mess and eliminating disorder.

False image

The authors compare the inadequacy of woman's choice in the social services with the seductive abundance of consumer goods with which she is showered. Far better, they say, to have more day nurseries, more play centres for children living in crowded city flats, more launderette services so that removable drudgery like the washing and ironing of clothes could be taken out of the home altogether, in short, more real freedom from chores than any number of gadget-ridden washing machines, cooking equipment and vacuum cleaners.

They are scathing on the subject of women's magazines, many of which portray a "false and perverted image of femininity and purvey a sentimental and superficial handling of women's problems." Woman, as woman in the home, forms the most important group of spenders today, controlling or directly influencing two-thirds of the country's consumer purchasing power, and this affects the whole ideological content of many women's magazines, which never seek to raise a woman's sights higher than the narrow confines of her home.

They attack the "agony columns" in such magazines, in which women are encouraged to think that difficulties are of their own making and that they bear sole responsibility for their solution.

Such advice, they claim, ignores the link between woman's problem and the social fabric of which she is part.

Night shifts

Mrs. Berger and Mrs. Maizels are angry about the quality of girls' education. They quote the Countess of Longford (formerly Lady Pakenham) who said: "All agree that boys should be educated as people, not as little generals, stockbrokers or farmers-to-be. Girls, however, are regarded as 'little women' before they are human beings."

They suggest further additions to the curriculum in preparing girls for their domestic role. "How does one interest girls in cleaning up dirt, making the beds, and scrubbing the kitchen floor?" they ask sardonically. "Perhaps by a really imaginative course which would train them for the more exciting aspects of home life? Spells of solitary confinement, for instance, to prepare for the loneliness of sub-topia; a course in body-building to be fit enough to push the pram, carry the shopping and pull up the hill the child who is too tired to pedal his tricycle.

"Night work shifts to train continual duty during teething trouble. For carrying coals, stoking up the boilers a[nd] ocean voyage down in the [?] would perhaps help."

This book is angry but not peevish. It makes b[?] criticisms where criticism[s] necessary, but it also has a structive and progressive app[?] to women's future. The au[?] are keenly aware of the ano[?] described by Dame Anne Go[?] general secretary of the Cle[?] and Administrative Wo[?] Union:

A paradox

"For my part it has always clear to me that being ab[?] earn and spend my own m[?] is a wonderful consolation fo[?] being offered a seat on a [?] she said.

"Our problem at this tim[?] not that we have too [?] emancipation but that the pr[?] has stopped short at a point v[?] we are in danger of getting worst of both worlds."

Mrs. Berger and Mrs. Ma[?] want women to be aware of and point out that it is a solution of the parado[?] economic affluence and [?] negligence that a new and diff[?] life for women depends.

The hat bar was a nove[l] Market at the City Hall, who found a bargain w[?] John's Cresce[nt]

an untrained nanny, to look after his three children. She also did the sewing and mending and probably the cooking on cook's day off. She was Miss Neale, and although she stayed with us many years we never called her anything else, and I cannot even remember her first name. From time to time she was visited by Gilbert, a man older than herself, who wanted to marry her. But her loyalty to the family was such that she rejected his continual offers. Eventually, when we were all at boarding school, she accepted and left, without any ceremony or golden handshake for all the years of her life she had devoted to our family. She just was not there when we returned from school for the holidays. I doubt if we learnt much from her except honesty and truth and the need to accept one's lot in life if not cheerfully then at least without a lot of fuss. I don't remember her smiling, but I suppose she must have done. I certainly never saw her smile at Gilbert.

Miss Neale was treated more or less as one of the family, but the other servants were regarded as inferior beings to be exploited to the full. Their rooms were periodically searched in case they had stolen anything. Special tea was bought for them – a lower grade – until my mother discovered that they were drinking the good and she was getting the poor. When my mother was 'off colour' either my sister, Joyce or I were deployed giving the servants their orders and reprimands. At the time, I rather fancied myself in the task, but later I became ashamed that a young girl with no experience, no training, and precious little idea of what life was really like should be allowed to lord it over hardworking and dedicated cooks and housemaids, who were giving their life to looking after a middleclass, uncaring family.

It was by no means uncommon for the daughters of relatively rich families to be given this kind of experience. It was all part of the preparation for marriage which parents saw as the only destiny for their daughters – not too soon, of course, around twenty-four or five, but not too late. Twenty-nine was around the old maid mark. By the time a girl was of marriageable age she would have learned how to buy clothes, which included getting the upper hand of the saleswoman, and how to shop for the family meals, cooking them and serving them. I was lucky. My mother soon realised that I was not going to play the marriage preparation game and she stopped trying to mould me into the daughter-hawking routine, but I learned the household skills which stood me in good stead in later life.

III
Life in
Boarding
School

NCCL Works for Women's Rights

For forty years, the National Council for Civil Liberties has fought against discrimination. It has supported, advised and campaigned for women, for minority groups and for individuals who have been denied legal and social rights.

This year, we set up a new women's rights group . . .

to campaign on laws affecting women —
we are lobbying for an effective anti-discrimination law and an end to discrimination against British women under the immigration rules; our model Anti-Discrimination law is the most comprehensive published in this country

to take up cases on behalf of women —
we can represent women at tribunals and in court; we have advised and helped hundreds of women, and we are taking as many cases as possible to the European Commission on Human Rights

to organise national and local activity —
our Women's Rights Conference brought together over 500 women from trade unions and the women's movement and is being followed by local evening and one-day meetings to initiate campaigns

to research the position of women —
current research projects cover social security and the immigration / nationality laws; reports are planned on protective legislation, education and training for girls, the legal rights of battered wives, and couples where the woman is the bread-winner.

If you think extending women's rights is a job worth doing, please help us do it. Get involved in the Anti-Discrimination campaign. Use our Conference report to organise local activity. And please send us a donation to keep the work going.

WHEN I WAS TWELVE it was time to go to secondary school, and that meant boarding school. Great discussions took place as to which school though the only real decision my father had to make as far as our schooling was concerned was how much he was prepared to pay. He chose middle price schools for us all: the fees were around forty pounds a term so his outlay was around five pounds a week since because of age differences only two of us were at school at any one time. It would be about the cost of the wages of two of his employees.

My father and my mother did not have to make major decisions about what type of schools we should go to. In the end, Lowther College was chosen partly because it was cheap, and partly because it was in north Wales, a part of the country known to us for holidays. No one in our social strata even thought of sending their children to state schools. They were for the indigent poor though I believe that my father would have sent us there had it not been for the social stigma he would have incurred. He himself went to what was called in his day a board school and in any case he considered education as of doubtful value beyond the three Rs. My sister Joyce and I went to a girls' preparatory school, and my brother Peter to a similar one for boys. Although we learned to read and write quite quickly none of us showed any academic strength or zeal. Questions of discipline did not arise. At home we did as we were told, and when we got to school this came naturally. By the time we were twelve our reactions were pretty automatic and we showed little initiative. We were priggish as well as snobbish, and we thought we were a good deal better than anyone else. We were very suitable for the type of minor 'public' boarding school to which we were sent in our twelfth year.

The first time I went to the boarding school I was taken by car.

It was 1926 and there was a general strike and I had to be content with a suitcase to hold my clothes although a large trunk was ready packed, which was too large to go inside the car and my father would not have it on the roof rack because he said it would incite striking railway men and we might be attacked.

I was a very young twelve and got lumbered with an even younger twelve through our mother's chattering. It blighted my first term but in the second term my prowess at games – hockey, lacrosse, tennis, and cricket – got me into a better set and from that time onwards I was what is laughingly called a 'leader'. I enjoyed school although the holidays were a bit of a nightmare for both me and my mother. We had few friends since our schools were miles away and the pupils scattered all over the north west of the country. At first, we had friends from our preparatory school days but gradually these friendships fell away. We were always glad to get back to school and have some companions of our own age.

I slithered through my school years, learning little and getting by because I was good at games. Because I was so good at games I was 'popular' and because I was never bright enough to be made prefect I had no responsibility and even no sense of responsibility. As I struggled into sixth form, such as it was, became the captain of most of the games teams, excelled at gymnastics and did as I was told, for most of the time my life ran smoothly. I failed most exams although by some miracle I managed to gain school certificates in my last year.

I left school a sports heroine – I played lacrosse and hockey at Junior County level, later golf – and though I had no other attributes, I had a very high opinion of myself, thinking I would continue to sail through life with the same popularity as I enjoyed at school. I did not have the wit to heed the warning given to me by a much older girl who came from South America and with whom I had a row when she told me that those who were popular at school were not necessarily either popular or successful when they went into the real world.

And so it turned out. My first few years after school were miserable because my expectations were quite out of line with my capabilities. I was ill-fitted for further education even if my father had allowed it. I was even less fitted to take part in the coffee morning, bridge playing, man-hunting life my parents thought was proper. I was nothing. And I was miserable.

For some time I suffered from an acute inferiority complex because of this. Most of my friends were at some sort of institution of further education but my father did not believe in girls learning anything except how to run a house and be a good wife. Nevertheless, I spent a great deal of time studying in the local library refusing to join in the dinner dances

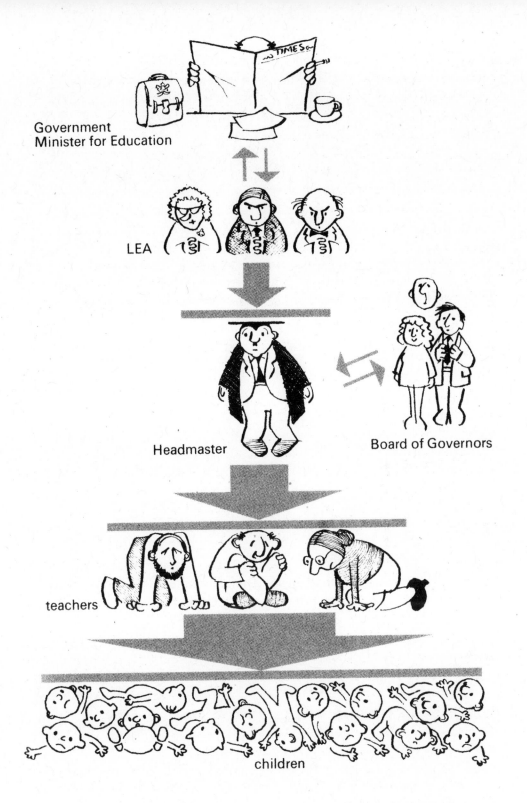

Government Minister for Education

LEA

Headmaster

Board of Governors

teachers

children

At the moment the power structure of most schools works something like this. But should the arrows be pointing the other way?

Schooldays • NANCIE WHITTAKER

I DIDN'T have to walk to school. When I woke up in the morning I was there already. It was that kind of a school. All the time I was there, with the possible exception of the first few weeks, when everything was a novelty, the thing I most wanted to do was just what I wasn't doing at the moment. If I were dressed in a blazer and fancy cap waiting for the opposing team to arrive and play us at hockey, I wanted to be arranging my foreign stamps, in spite of the fact that I had looked forward to this match for weeks, and if I were reading a book I wanted to finish it so that I could read another one. All the time my mind was wandering from the task in hand to some future undertaking.

All the week I resented the glaringly obvious time-tables that hung in the classrooms and bade me do this at three o'clock, and the other at four o'clock, and never have any time to myself until Sunday came round, and I wondered whose bloomer had placed this day at my disposal, when I did not know what to do with it.

I wondered at the system which forced friendships with those not quite contemporary to be degrading or sentimental, and although it added an extra spice to a monotonous routine, it raised a million doubts in my mind, when I wasn't actually at school, as to the value of friendships with one's elders or youngers. In the presence of the former I felt inferior, and I looked down on the latter.

In the monotonous run of the day—breakfast, walk, lessons, dinner, games, lessons, tea, prep., supper, bed—we clung to any small thing that would relieve it. Things like the temper of a mistress, the behaviour of

individuals towards one another became immensely important, and I remember wishing week after week for a whole term that the procedure adopted by one chef who had been dismissed for his ' fancy ways ' of putting chopped parsley in the soup and tomato sauce in the fish cakes could be repeated.

I regarded lessons as times for amusement at the expense of the softer-hearted mistresses, and even went as far as to think it clever when I was told that, although I was not physically lazy, I certainly was mentally. It seemed to be then a hard-earned distinction. Games I worshipped and shelved everything for them. The school was run on the assumption that a girl who didn't like games was either mentally or physically deficient, lazy or immoral, and so the urge to play games well was fostered, not only by the popularity it brought, but by a desire to be considered none of these things.

Mob fever controlled all opinion. Everyone thought the same thing at the same time, but it only took the strength of one average mind with influence to turn the whole 250 girls round to a completely opposite viewpoint. What the upper ten thought at teatime, the mob had adopted by the time they went to bed.

Bed was the most perfect thing in school life, and the desire for more sleep saved my parents a great deal of money, as the reason I gave up taking music lessons was that once a week we had to rise half an hour early and practise the piano before breakfast.

The world we lived in was so complete in itself, so self-contained, that it never occurred to me that there was anything outside the walls which surrounded the park. For me, it just didn't exist ; and, in spite of the holidays, which I regarded as a nuisance when they were a reality and a godsend during term time, I was totally disinterested in anything I saw reported in the papers, which I regarded as daily entertainment for the masses rather than a slant on everyday affairs.

Not for a moment did I imagine that school was a preparation for later days. When I didn't regard it as a respite for parents, I thought it was probably a convention so ingrained that it couldn't be relaxed, and history and geography were taught because, after all, you had to do something when you weren't playing hockey or tennis. I can remember thinking that it did not seem much good learning arithmetic and algebra, when what you really wanted to know was how to keep a room full of people amused. It was the one thing to despise school and ' long for the holidays,' and rather than be thought abnormal I, too, ' longed for the holidays ' in public when, actually, I disliked them, partly because I never knew quite how to fill in my time and partly because the self-importance I was gathering every term was shaken from me at home.

The longer I stayed at school the more self-important I became, until, when I left, I was so puffed up by this pseudo self-assurance that it was

difficult for me to believe that I had my own way to make if I were to be noticed at all. I imagined that because I was among the intelligent upper ten at school I should take my place automatically among the somebodies in the world. Incidentally, I consider this one of the systems of public schools : to give their pupils the idea that they count.

I realise now how I wasted my time, how little I learnt, not even enough to realise how little I should ever know. I realise that whatever I learnt was unconsciously picked up from the principal of the school as a woman and not as a teacher. I realise I wasn't helped to grasp that life was not all social activity. I thank goodness that I met all types, all classes, all colours, but I regret I never saw clearly that anyone who doesn't put into the stockpot of the world as much, if not more, than they take out is a parasite.

– morning coffee in cafés – clothes buying – husband hunt routines –
and this isolated me from the family and from friends. I think my parents
were rather ashamed of me. I was not their idea of an ideal daughter. One
thing did please them. On a boat trip to Marseille and back on a P&O
steamer going to the Far East I had my first love affair. I was 17 and the
ship's doctor was the man who fell in love with me. I don't think I was
in love with him but I did my best. After he came back from the Far East
he came to see me but by this time I had found another boyfriend, and
he had to be consoled by my mother.

I had one saving grace. I had a lot of common sense. I learned it
not only from my parents in my early years but from the principal of my
boarding school, a Mrs Lindley who, with her husband Dr Lindley, owned
the school. She had no academic training or qualifications, leaving such
matters to her headmistress, a soulful spinster, as were the rest of the staff.
As hard as they tried to drive a bit of learning into 300 girls from the lower
middle-class, she worked harder at telling them that success in life
depended on not what they knew but what they could do. She was a lover
of good food and thought the love of food made better cooks than lessons
in domestic science. The food we ate at school was rather extraordinary.
Cream with our porridge or cornflakes. We had Welsh lamb seasoned with
rosemary, raw tomatoes and grated nuts, egg mayonnaise with home made
mayonnaise, rare roast beef, crisp roast potatoes, many fresh vegetables
and no stodgy puddings. The staff ate with the girls, including Mrs Lindley
and her husband, at whose table a different set of girls sat every day. The
conversation there ranged from a discussion of food, the importance of
choosing the right clothes for the right occasion, to the necessity of girls
having interests and, where appropriate, jobs outside the home.

The Lindleys had no children of their own but they befriended many
children whose circumstances were less favourable than they thought they
ought to be. Many years after I left I met Mrs Lindley in a London street.
She was dressed as she always was, in a smart frockcoat (as we used to
call them) which could be worn outside in mild weather and was a rather
heavy woollen frock with pockets and collar which made it look a bit like
a coat. Hers reached beyond her mid-calf. She told me she was looking
for a job to help the war effort but no government department seemed at
all interested. She was both astonished and enraged as she was offering
her services without payment. She was a good organiser and could have
been extremely useful. Later I had word that she had returned to Wales,
where her mock castle school stood as imposing as ever, now half empty,
a disappointed woman.

Who's keeping an eye on them while they're keeping an eye on you?

civil liberty

IV
Après School

Above A penny dinner for board school children in 1885.
Below 'Meat and two veg' at a Kent school in the forties.

los derechos de los niños

A. S. Neill / Paul Adams / Leila Berg / Nan Berger
Michael Duane / Robert Ollendorff

extemporáneos ⊕ el viento cambia

FOR MORE THAN two years after I left school
I swanned around doing the sort of things acceptable to my parents.
I wore fancy clothes, used a lot of make up and went to the hairdressers
regularly, met my friends for morning coffee in posh cafés, went to dances,
parties and was generally idle and available. In spite of it all the young
men I attracted – and there were not too many – were not quite what my
parents or myself thought suitable for marriage. Except for one. He was a
homosexual and I loved him dearly. I don't think my parents realised what
his sexual inclinations were. They thought he was just very charming.

He had many contacts in the theatre so whenever we went to a play
we went backstage and I met quite a few people whom I would otherwise
not have done. One of them was David Webster who was to become the
administrator of Covent Garden. At that time he was either the buyer or
the manager of the bargain basement of the late Lord Woolton's Retail
Emporium in Liverpool, and in his spare time he produced Shakespeare
in the open air in Wallasey Park. His acute sense of humour made the
after-theatre supper parties he gave at the Adelphi Hotel a rare treat
– good food and wine and exciting talk, not the beer swilling necking
parties I was used to.

It was perhaps the contact with people like David Webster, slight
though it was, which helped me realise that the life I was leading in the
sterile town of Southport was useless and a bit immoral. The town was
sterile because it was really a dormitory for Liverpool and Manchester,
and there was practically no industry there and consequently very few
working-class people. I was just one of thousands of middle-class girls
marking time until they found a suitable husband, or had one found for
them, which was a worse prospect. My only fixed chore of the day was

to meet my father at the station where he arrived at around 5.30 pm from Manchester to which he commuted every weekday.

At this time, one of the joys of my life was driving my father's two litre Bentley. With his brother, eighteen years younger, my father had bought two Bentley chassis in 1924. Their numbers were 126 and 128. These two cars were run for months just as chassis – that is how performance cars were bought in those days, with bucket-seats for the driver and one passenger. They had makeshift windscreens and I can see my mother now with goggles and helmeted head start off on one tour or another. Both my father and mother covered thousands of miles with two cars in this condition. Later we had a body built on to ours, a sort of four-seater taxi-like contraption built by skilled hands working for several months. When we had learned to drive, our first task was to take my father to the station and then collect him and to take my mother shopping if she wished. As most things were delivered, even her clothes – on approval – to the door and collected when she had made her choice, this was a rare outing.

As compensation for fetching and carrying for my father, I was allowed to take the Bentley out on my own from time to time. In the days when I was 'courting', the possession of a car was a great advantage – many of my minor affairs had more to do with the Bentley than with my charm.

Our household was not a very happy one. My father settled down with his whisky the moment he came in from the office and continued drinking all evening with a break for dinner. His arrival home was a signal for everyone to metaphorically stand to attention. Any visitors were bustled out and the activity in the house, such as it was, stopped unless it were directly connected with my father. His presence in the house was like a blanket, damping everything down. As children we were terrified of him and as we got older we began to realise that our mother was too.

The fear of my father must have been very deep in me and it lasted until it was replaced by contempt. I despised him for his anti-semitism; for his ruthless dealings with people, especially those he employed; and I loathed him for his rich friends. In the main these friends were men who gambled heavily in cotton futures, a thing my father never did, and who dropped into the house after the day's dealings, boasting of the thousands they had made. On the days they lost they stayed away. Questioning this acquisition of quick money and seeing so many able-bodied unemployed men sitting on their heels on street corners started me thinking about how society was organised. It was probably the first time I had made any real intellectual effort, and it was painful. About the same time, in 1933 when I was nineteen years old, still almost childlike in my thoughts, the Nazis set fire to the Reichstag and blamed the arson on the Communists. At the time the news of the fire hardly registered with me but later in the year when the four people accused of the arson were put on trial in Leipzig and the proceedings began to filter into the British papers, I began to take more notice.

One of the four accused was Dimitrov, a Bulgarian revolutionary who at the time of the fire was working underground in Germany. His cross-examination of Goering, the second most important person in the Nazi hierarchy, whom the prosecution had put in the witness box at a stage when the case was going badly for them, electrified the court with his exposure of the nature of Nazism and his defence of communism and the Soviet Union, a country comprising one sixth of the world.

The reports in the British press electrified me and I can remember asking my brother, then only seventeen and not long out of school, who this Dimitrov was. 'One of the most important men in European politics,' he snapped 'and you should be ashamed of yourself for not knowing about him.' I began to feel very ashamed at my lack of knowledge not only of people like Dimitrov but of almost everything else outside my tiny, protected, middle-class world. I wonder now how my brother was so much more au fait with world affairs than myself, although I was two years older. I suppose it was because in those days boys were better educated than girls and were expected to read newspapers and discuss what was going on in the world whereas girls were expected to not read newspapers or 'bother their heads' with serious matters.

The court performance of Dimitrov was a remarkable achievement. He had been in gaol for over five months, shackled day and night, during which time he worked in perfecting his German and his knowledge of German criminal law. He conducted his case better than the best lawyers could have done. Up until the time of the Reichstag fire trial my friends had been mainly people who thought politics was something that happened at general elections. You voted and that was the end of it. Most of them voted for a candidate rather than for a party or a policy. Their choice was between Liberal and Tory and whichever candidate caught their fancy, they voted for him. There were not many 'hers' standing as parliamentary candidates and had there been any they would not have collected any votes in my town in the thirties.

The Reichstag fire trial changed everything in my life. It changed my choice of friends and it changed my outlook. From that time on I finally turned my back on being one of thousands of girls in the town who led useless, pleasure seeking lives, whose activities depended on always having a current boyfriend to take them to dances, parties, acting

DON'T BE A MORAL COWARD

By NANCIE E. WHITTAKER

ONE repeatedly hears people asking others to do small things for them, such as asking the price of an article in a shop, inquiring the way, or obtaining some other information. If one asks the reason, they reply, "I didn't like to do it myself."

These same people would tackle a larger job with the utmost efficiency if it were necessary, but when it comes to these everyday insignificant incidents they fight shy.

All through their lives they leave undone or permit others to do these small things which they really wish they could do themselves with better grace.

These moral cowards refuse to make complaints in restaurants; instead they suffer bad service and come away disgruntled with a vow never to return; they refrain from returning unsatisfactory goods to shops, and then blame the shop when they have not given the vendors a chance to amend.

Every time a person neglects to do one of these jobs he is only widening the barrier that stands between him and mental peace. He refuses to ask questions to which he does not know the answers in case he should be thought ignorant. Instead of comparing himself with fellow men, he compares himself with the *Encyclopaedia Britannica*!

Day after day such folk allow buildings, events, and people to pass under their noses because they refuse to ask questions. Consequently they miss interesting information and many amusing incidents.

The only way to rid oneself of this moral cowardice is to grasp every opportunity of asking questions and accustoming oneself to deal with awkward situations, instead of pushing such matters on to others.

Go out of your way to talk to unknown people, and when you feel the urge to do a thing, do not hesitate to do it.

This may seem mentally fatiguing at first, but it quickly becomes natural, and you soon forget you were ever a moral coward.

as partners at the badminton club and the golf club. I sought friends outside my own middle-class group, I tried to educate myself by reading regularly in the local library and I studied the newspapers, the *Manchester Guardian* which I bought myself and the *Daily Mail* which was delivered to the house, my father's choice.

My family gave me very little encouragement saying it was all really a pose. I remember when I played my first bought classical record on our 'antique' cabinetted wind-up gramaphone, I was accused of showing off. It was a piano concerto by Rachmaninov, not exactly highbrow. Many years later when I played the same record to a working-class friend of mine who was very keen on music he poured scorn on it as 'café' music. I never did develop much understanding of classical music and to this day it plays little part in my life, unlike the love of jazz which does play a large part in my life, though I still stick to early Duke Ellington, Jelly Roll Morton, Bix Beiderbecke, the Dorsey Brothers, Dizzy Gillespie, Charlie Parker, Sidney Bechet, and the like. The 78 rpm records of these musicians are my tipple, augmented by the songs of Bertolt Brecht and Kurt Weill.

In our house there were plenty of rooms on the top floor, and I appropriated one, decorated it in dead white distemper and furnished it with odd pieces I bought in second hand shops. My brother did the same. At the time he needed a place to study as he had already embarked on his ploy of wanting to be a doctor to get out of my father's business where he had started to work as soon as he left school. My needs were different. I needed a place where I could be my new self. Since I had no qualifications of any kind finding a job was unlikely and in any case my parents would not have allowed it. Having a daughter who worked for a living was not far off the disgrace of having a prostitute in the family.

A job being impossible – or so I thought at the time – I decided that I would try my hand at writing. That would be an acceptable pastime to my father, who would regard it as a hobby. I wrote a good deal in those days nearly all of it unpublished and indeed unpublishable. I started a book on 'domestic service through the ages', I wrote a play about a homosexual man, and many articles with titles like 'Don't be a moral coward' – which I was myself. This was one of the ones which got published, probably because it was at least authentic. Why I did not just go and get a job in a shop or as a filing clerk I don't know. I suppose my fear of antagonising my parents was too great or because in spite of my changed outlook I was still too much of a snob to get an 'ordinary' job.

As I recall it now the coming to power of Hitler seemed almost my own private worry. No one talked about it or deplored it – except my brother. Young as he was he was the only person I knew who viewed the world as a whole. He had spent a year at Cambridge and made many political friends who widened his view of life. One of the friends he made was Boris Ord, the organist at King's, who often invited us both to supper in his flat with a grand semi-circular window in the main college building. He took us also into King's College Chapel late at night and played for us for half an hour or so.

In April 1934 my brother invited one of his girlfriends Phyllis and myself to spend a weekend in London with him and one of the 'outings' he took us on was a demonstration against Oswald Mosley's British Union of Fascists which was staging a meeting in the Royal Albert Hall, which held 10,000 people. I knew about the BUF and had even attended a meeting in Southport because one of my boyfriends decided to join. So, I was ready for the violence and danger. Phyllis who had never attended any kind of political meeting was not. At the first sight of the hundreds of policemen, on foot and mounted, jostling the crowd, she screamed. When we got pinned against some railings in a cul-de-sac by a posse of mounted police, she screamed even louder and had to be sent home. The police seemed more anxious to battle with the demonstrators yelling anti-fascist slogans outside than they were to restrain the Blackshirts who were given free rein to beat up people asking hostile questions inside. It all made me very frightened but I did not scream, already aware that screaming was about as useful as a tin full of bent nails.

The behaviour of the police was so awful that the National Council of Civil Liberties decided to set up its own enquiry, inviting those who had been present to write in about their experiences. Part of the letter I wrote to NCCL was as follows:

The first shocking behaviour I saw was the arrest of a man and his being dragged along between two mounted police, each holding one arm. Perhaps he deserved to be arrested but he certainly did not deserve such brutal treatment [...] Later we were standing against the railings in Thurloe Square listening to the anti-fascist speakers when the police charged us, using their white sticks. At least one man had a very bad head wound. We were unhurt but very frightened. The police eventually broke up the meeting and turned their attention to a march of protesters moving along Kensington Road. Protesters were shouting 'Red United Front' and one man in particular was taunting the police, calling them pro-fascist. He was dragged off by the police who beat him with their sticks. It was noticeable that the police did not harass those who were well dressed and looked as though they belonged to the area but they harassed others walking on the pavement by riding their horses at them and causing them to fall in heaps.

Back in Southport after my London visit I continued to read avidly but I was still slithering through life, alternating periods of hope that I would be successful with my writing with longer periods of despair that I wouldn't.

It was not until I was twenty-one, in 1935, that the first part of my life ended. My mother made it possible for me to leave home. I changed the comfort of a middle-class prosperous home for a bedsit in Bloomsbury. Not only did the days alter but the nights took on a different meaning. Nights and days ran into one another. Thinking started when meetings started, which was generally around 7pm, and did not end until meetings or discussions terminated which could be around 3am. Why the period after midnight had suddenly become so attractive puzzled me. Getting up at ten o'clock in the morning – possible for the unemployed, students and those who did not mind having their wages docked an hour or two on occasions – seemed to have a special attraction. Late nights and late rising offended my puritan feelings, and it took a long time to get over the feeling that it was not only totally unnecessary but also pretty slovenly and certainly counter-productive.

Looking at my achievements between leaving school and leaving London I can see very few obvious wins and quite a few no scores. I did not please my parents by making what might be described as a good marriage. I did not go to university and obtain a reasonable degree. I did not follow up on my early prowess at sports although I did become quite a good golfer. The only achievement of this first phase of my life was to develop some common sense, to reject the traditional middle class conventions of conservative commitment without throwing out what was positive in the liberal tradition.

There are lots of other phrases like 'right of way', everyday language is full of them. Here are a few:

Serves her right

He is standing on his rights

I know my rights

I had a perfect right to do it

In her own right

They all mean slightly different things but the number of times you hear people use these phrases suggests that we take our many different rights rather seriously. We consider that rights bring advantages and feel aggrieved when we are deprived of them.

Children's rights

Paul Adams

Leila Berg

Nan Berger

Michael Duane

A S Neill

Robert Ollendorff

towards the liberation of the child

V
Evaluating Capitalism

Under surveillance: protection or intrusion?

RIGHTS

A Handbook for People under Age
NAN BERGER

I WAS BEGINNING TO look at what was happening around me in a more scientific way. Looking back, I remember the conversations I had heard in my father's house during the 1931 crisis. Men who gambled in cotton futures came to visit my father, wringing their hands and saying the world would never be the same again. Their way of life was threatened. They feared they might have to do some real work, in order to exist. They rejoiced that the Labour government had fallen and that Ramsay McDonald had virtually crossed over to their side, and they applauded the plans to cut wages and unemployment benefits. They looked with fear at the groups of unemployed men who hung about at street corners or sat on their haunches and played cards on the pavement. The proper place for working men was at work, they thought, and it made them uneasy to see men doing nothing. They were very class conscious, my father especially so.

It all confirmed what I already believed about capitalism being a wicked system needing to be replaced. It all seemed so simple. If enough people opposed capitalism it would be defeated and some other, fairer, type of system would come into being. That is what I thought until I began to study Marx and the other socialist writers. I then began to see why I should have listened more carefully to what my father's friends said about the way society should be organised. They knew what they wanted, and what they had to do to get it and retain it. I could not say the same about myself.

Gradually, through study, I was able to argue the case for socialism in a more convincing manner. But it was by no means easy. One had to be well versed not only in the theoretical basis for socialism but also in the political situation in other countries. Information was hard to get. It came mainly from news agencies. News on the radio was not too plentiful and there was of course no television. So, to be able to understand what was happening in, say, South America one had to do a large amount of reading. I found then, as I find now, that the *Daily Telegraph* had the best coverage of news. It was, of course, heavily biased towards the right but once you knew the way of its bias you could understand what had actually happened. I found keeping ahead with world politics a hard job. After all I was only partially educated myself, I was inexperienced and untravelled. I faced better minds at a disadvantage. My inferiority complex did not allow me to take chances with facts.

By 1935, if not before, my existence in Southport with its unbalanced population – it was and probably still is populated largely by people who earned their living elsewhere – had become quite meaningless. My father persisted in his view that women should be at home mending socks and underpants and would not hear of my taking a job. He could have helped me to get something even though I had no qualifications other than a diploma in horticulture but his pride would not let him.

My escape to London – the great metropolis northerners knew nothing about – had to be fudged just as Peter's departure to Cambridge and later to the London School of Economics had to be engineered on lines which were not strictly honest. He had started his working life at the warehouse owned by my father. For six months, he lugged bales of gunny onto lorries, quarrelling with my father when he had the energy. When it came time for him to be upgraded to office work he told my father that he had a great ambition to be a doctor and wanted to go to Cambridge to study. It was the only sort of proposition which would have cut any ice with my father. Any plea to go to university on general educational grounds would have been rejected. The dedicated doctor ploy worked and off he went to study and sit for his preliminary examinations. He was off the hook and by the time he failed his first MB, he was able to slide off to London and the LSE, arguing that a degree in economics would help him in the family business – another bit of faking because my father needed an economist about as much as he needed a hole in the head. I don't think he even knew what an economist was. He probably thought it was a sort of glorified bookkeeper. Nor had my brother any intention of returning to the family fold. Once the chain was slackened it was easy to slip it, and from that point on his links with the family became less strong. Like all good businessmen my father knew when to make a virtue out of necessity and boasted about his clever son who had gained a place at a university which in those days was no great feat provided one could pay the fees – but my father was too ignorant to know this.

It was mother who engineered my lucky escape. She knew that
I too should have gone to university but that was something my father
would not swallow. Having left school at twelve himself and starting his
own business by the time he was eighteen, employing his own father and
brother, he considered that higher education was totally unnecessary for
anyone, and for girls it was unthinkable. She came up with the idea that
Peter needed someone to look after him in London and that I could fulfil
this role well. She knew it was a fudge but my father accepted it and
agreed to give me an allowance of four pounds a week, the same as
he gave to Peter.

He insisted that we had to live in a proper flat. No child of my father
could live in a student bedsit. The flat he chose was in Clare Court, near
Kings Cross Station, a newly built block with central heating, fitted
kitchen and fridge thrown in. The rent was more than we could really
afford on our joint income of eight pounds a week but we managed well
enough even though we occasionally had to pawn our watches. We were
a lot better off than most people – at the time the average wage in industry
was around two pounds a week.

Even before we left home we had begun to question the principles
on which we were brought up which were roughly that the poor were
poor because they did not want to work and that anyone could be well off
if they put enough effort into making money. That was my father's official
view, and to back it up he had his own experience. In fact, he knew that
without the poor he could not be rich. By this time, he was employing
about 150 men and women, most of them unskilled.

I well remember the time when one middle-aged woman who did odd
chores about the warehouse including mashing tea for the other workers
was given a bit more responsibility. After a couple of weeks, she asked for
her old job back. 'I get no time for crocheting,' she said. She could earn
more than her miserable rise by making crocheted mats to sell in the
market on a Saturday afternoon.

When I arrived in London I had the advantage of Peter's political
connections at LSE and more or less stepped into the successful national
campaign, led by the Communist Party, against cuts in unemployment
benefits.

At this time the dues paying membership of the Communist Party
was about 7,700 but the sales of the *Daily Worker* were 30,000 daily,
rising to 70,000 at the weekend. Selling to people at tube stations, factory
gates, outside cinemas was, I discovered later, the number one job for
party members and party supporters. My first sales pitch was in Central
London on Jubilee day, 6 May 1935, the twenty-fifth anniversary of the

DAILY WORKER, MAY 7, 1935.

TERRIBLE MINE DISASTER

(See Page 2)

Workers of the World, Unite!

DAILY WORKER

ORGAN OF THE COMMUNIST PARTY OF GREAT BRITAIN (SECTION OF COMMUNIST INTERNATIONAL)

Wage Cuts For Fishermen

(See Page 3)

No. 1657 | REGISTERED AT THE G.P.O. AS A NEWSPAPER | TUESDAY, MAY 7, 1935 | One Penny

JOLT FOR JUBILEE PARADE

Drama Of Red Banner Across The Royal Route

BIGSHOTS FLAUNT IN IMPERIAL SPREE

WITH the capitalist Press in a frenzy of high-paid enthusiasm, the upper-classes —slightly woozy after an all-night spree in the West End—flag-wagging in the expensive seats along the route, and a mixed bag of the Provincial bourgeoisie presenting a rear view to the line of route as they tried to see the doings in mirrors held above their heads, the rulers of the British Empire staged their super-demonstration in London yesterday.

The crowds, in some places huge, in others very thin, saw cavalry and artillery trotting by in full dress uniform—perhaps the last time anyone will see that in London streets, for in the next war golden epaulettes will not be worn, and those lances with the pretty pennants on them will not be in use against the poison-gas bombs and the flame-throwers.

They saw the King and the Queen for a moment or two, moving rapidly past in ornate coaches with poker-faced lackeys looking like something out of Madame Tussaud's or figures in one of those old films of Russia when the Tsar still ruled.

They saw the bigshots to whom these 25 years have brought power and honour.

They saw the notorious Maharajahs, with "Mr. A" riding in pompous glory past the Law Courts, whence the reek of his habits and customs once floated through the world.

Then, in Fleet Street, occurred the most sensational episode of the route.

Suddenly a huge banner, stretched across the street and inscribed "Long May They Reign," unfolded and revealed above the heads of the astounded assembly and the dropping jaws of the massed police a huge hammer and sickle.

On each side of the great opened banner flamed east and west along Fleet Street the slogans:—

"WORKERS OF ALL LANDS, UNITE!"

And on the other:—

"TWENTY-FIVE YEARS OF HUNGER AND WAR."

STORY BEHIND THE BANNER

Befooled Police Helped Fix It

BIGSHOTS riding in pomp, massed splits turned out to guard the route, the high-powered scribes and trained seals of the capitalist Press massing the windows of Fleet Street, gaped and gasped when suddenly across the very route of the Royal cavalcade an apparently loyal banner underwent a strange transformation and revealed the symbol of workers' power, and the slogans of the workers floating in the brilliant sun.

Only later was revealed the uproarious fact that a few hours before the befooled police had themselves actually assisted the placing of the banner across the street, and had held up the traffic of Fleet Street in order to allow it to be swung into place.

Behind the placing of that banner lies an extraordinary story of workers' ingenuity and determination.

Late yesterday afternoon a DAILY WORKER reporter heard the amazing facts from a worker who gave no name but had rung up to tell us that if we wanted the story behind the banner we could get it.

The huge banner was made in such a way that it could be hung across the street with nothing visible on it but loyal "Gawd Save" slogans stretching along either side. At a touch, the loyal slogans would—in every sense of the word—flop, and as the banner unfurled it would display instead the hammer and sickle and the slogans of the workers.

Two offices in Fleet Street were selected as the places between which it was to be hung across the Royal route.

Then came a series of episodes which remind one of the famous story of the Captain of Koepenick, the masquerader, who fooled a whole town because the people in it were drunk with enthusiasm and reverence for anything in uniform.

The gentlemen in the Fleet Street offices received on Sunday afternoon a telephone call supposedly from the Office of Works.

Would they, the alleged Office of Works asked, be able to keep open long enough for a final banner to be hung across Fleet Street from their first floor window to complete the decorations for the Jubilee?

In a frenzy of patriotic enthusiasm they said they would stay all night if necessary.

When the workers arrived with the banner they found everyone only too delighted to assist, with no questions asked because all present were woozy with the Jubilee dope.

As the banner began to be slung across the street police and car owners co-operated to hold up the traffic.

A marching band of young bourgeois in evening clothes parading the streets stopped and cheered wildly.

And after an hour or so of hard work, in full view of several score police and a large assortment of capitalist journalists, the banner was firmly in [illegible], the release device fixed and the workers safely departed.

Red Banner Dropped

International Sung At Service

(From Our Worker Correspondent)

BRIGHTON, Monday. — At the thanksgiving service at Preston Park a group of workers sang the "International," and called for three cheers for the Soviet Union.

As the procession passed under the viaduct on its way to the sea-front, a large red banner, 18 ft. long unfurled from the viaduct with the inscription:—

"25 Years of Hunger and War."

Slogans Shouted

"Twenty-five years of hunger," and such slogans were shouted by workers in Ludgate Circus as the Royal procession passed that point.

Balloons Dropped

Immediately the Royal procession passed there were balloons released from a building in Charing Cross with luggage labels tied to them with slogans explaining the war preparations behind the Jubilee and the wage-cuts and the Means Test.

One minute after they had been released the police were racing upstairs in the building, but nobody was found by them.

NO ROAD FOR LANDLORDS

In a working-class street in Manchester, where the houses were almost covered with bunting, a large notice had been put up:—

"This road is closed to landlords. Rent spent."

Parasites' Jubilee

"Jubilee for Parasites—Means Test for Workers" was the big white slogan painted on the ramp facing the Chelsea Embankment.

The fire brigade was called out to whitewash it over, but not before it had been responsible for much favourable comment.

Red Builders

Building workers on the Wynn's job, Park Royal, who had demanded to work and did, hoisted the Red Flag with the hammer and sickle on it yesterday.

United Front

A Labour Party member assisted the N.U.W.M. in the running of a meeting for the purpose of exposing the Jubilee celebrations at the Triangle, Peckham. He was particularly strong in replying to some hecklers who had gathered around.

One Flag

Dublin was a sea of contempt for the King. There was one Union Jack flying from Trinity College, and that was only kept flying through the employment of a large force of police going on duty in relays.

"SYMBOLS OF SUBJECTION"

The following resolution was sent yesterday morning to Mr. Dulanty, Free State High Commissioner in London.

"Irish Republican exiles in London resent and repudiate the countenance and support given by the representatives of Irish Free State Government here to the imperialist Jubilee celebrations which are being staged in an attempt to rouse the feeling of the British workers in preparation for the blood bath of another war, and by the same forces which are waging an economic war on the Irish Free State with the purpose of breaking Republican resistance and so securing Ireland as a base in that war.

"The display among the symbols of subjection to imperialism, of the tricolours under which Republicans died in the fight against British imperialism, by the representatives of the Free State Government, at a time when the farmers and working people of the Free State are suffering acute hardship in resisting British attack, is a betrayal of the people bearing the brunt of the economic war, a betrayal of Irish Republican traditions and Republican spirit, a misrepresentation of the feelings of the Irish people, and a proof that the Government has gone out of the leadership of the Republican fight and that Republican forces must regroup under a real Republican leadership in the fight for freedom."

The resolution is signed by Sean Mulgrew and Charles Donnelly (on behalf of the London Council of the Republican Congress), and Joseph H. Fowler (president of the Roger Casement Sinn Fein Club, London).

GLASGOW'S JUBILEE PROTEST

Over 1,000 March Through Streets

(From Our Own Correspondent)

GLASGOW, Monday.

OVER 1,000 workers marched through the main street in Glasgow as a protest against the Jubilee celebrations.

Prior to the demonstration starting off from Glasgow Green, Harry McShane addressed the meeting, thus breaking the ban imposed by the police.

Following the march through the street, which was witnessed by many thousands, the anti-Jubilee demonstrators massed at Hanover Street and their ranks were swollen by another 1,000 workers. There was no interference by the police.

The meeting was addressed by Comrades McShane, Kerrigan, Hart and a young girl, with Gerrard presiding.

The demonstration through the streets was led by the Maryhill flute band and there was good slogan-shouting en route.

The demonstration was organised by the Communist Party, and the I.L.P. leaders did not participate.

In glaring contrast Glasgow's Labour majority sent an address of warmest congratulation to the King, but their patriotism did not extend to giving a holiday to the painters cleaning the Council Chamber or extra wages to the transport employees sweltering and sweating in making possible the exodus of the city workers to the outlying open spaces and holiday centres.

Welsh Women Getting Ready

LABOUR DAY, organised by the S.W.M.F. throughout South Wales yesterday, took the nature of anti-Jubilee demonstrations in several places, particularly in those where preparations are going ahead to muster strong contingents of women for the protest march into Cardiff on May 10, the eve of the day when the Prince of Wales visits Cardiff for the Jubilee celebrations.

Every mining town and village had its demonstration or meeting.

The character of the demonstrations can be seen from the one which took place in Bedlinog, a small mining village.

Here over 200 workers marched through the streets singing the "Red Flag" and the "International."

During the next few days there will be intense activity in preparation for the March into Cardiff of the working women from the mining villages of South Wales and Monmouthshire.

Recruiting has been steadily going on, and the 500 marchers aimed at by the organisers will take the road as the standard bearers of revolt against the Jubilee ballyhoo and place their demands before the Prince of Wales.

Financial assistance is urgently needed

Send your donation to the Joint Secretary, 47, Commercial Street, Nantymoel, Glamorgan.

NEW PHASE IN SOVIET UNION

Stalin's Appeal For More Skilled Workers

From Our Own Correspondent, W. G. SHEPHERD

MOSCOW, Monday.

"BEFORE, we used to say: 'Technique decides everything.' But now the emphasis must be put on the people, on the cadres of workers who have to master technique. That is why the old slogan, 'technique decides everything,' reflecting a period already passed, when we experienced hunger in the field of technique, must now be substituted by a new slogan: 'Cadres decide everything.'"

So said Stalin, speaking at the graduation ceremony of students of the Military Academy yesterday, when a new detachment of engineers and technicians joined the ranks of the Workers' and Peasants' Red Army.

The Soviet Union has built its industrial plant; the need is now for the highly-trained workers, specialists, etc., to get the best out of what has been achieved.

By far the greatest number of the graduates are going to the industrial plants and laboratories of the scientific institutes.

GREAT SUCCESSES

Comrade Stalin emphasised the great successes made by the Soviet Union both in the field of industrial production and of industrial management.

"You all know that we received as a legacy from the past a technically backward and impoverished country, a country ruined by four years of imperialist war and by three years of civil war, a country with a semi-literate population, with a low technique, with small patches of industry in a sea of small peasant farmsteads.

"Our great task was to switch the country from the rails of the Middle Ages and ignorance to the rails of modern industry and mechanised agriculture. As you have seen it has been a serious and difficult task.

"There were no machines for industry. There were no machines for agriculture. There were no machines for transport. We had not even the elementary technical basis without which the industrial transformation of the country was inconceivable.

INDUSTRY, AGRICULTURE, TRANSPORT

"First-class industry had to be created. This industry had to be directed along lines such that it was capable of reorganising not only itself, but also agriculture and our railway transport.

"This entailed sacrifices on our part and the most rigorous economy in everything. We had to economise on food, on schools, on textiles in order to accumulate the necessary means for creating our industrial basis.

"There was no other way of eliminating our hunger in the field of technical development.

"This is what Lenin taught us, and we have followed Lenin's footsteps.

"We had to arm ourselves with strong nerves, Bolshevist firmness and stubborn patience in order to overcome the first failures, and steadfastly to march forward towards our great aim, admitting neither vacillation nor uncertainty within our ranks.

HOW WE FOUGHT

"You know that we conducted our struggle in just this way.

"Those comrades who were frightened by the difficulties before us said: 'What do we need with your industrialisation and collectivisation, your machines, tractors, combines, motor-cars? You would do much better to give us more textile, you would do better to buy more raw materials for the production of articles for general consumption, and should give our people more of all these minor things which make the life of people pleasant. In our state of backwardness the creation of first-class industry is a dangerous dream.'

"This also would have been a 'plan,' but under such a 'plan' we should have had no metal industry,

(Continued on Page Four)

781 Postal Delegates In Conference

(From Our Correspondent)

PORTHCAWL, Monday.—There are seven hundred and eighty-one delegates at the sixteenth annual conference of the Union of Post Office Workers, which opened to-day in Porthcawl.

Mr. Dunster, in his chairman's address, said that since the annual conference last year important changes have taken place. The Union does not oppose developments, believing that such changes can be accepted with parallel improvements of the conditions of the staff. The community must not only be concerned with the benefits which they have got, but also with conditions resulting from the concessions.

The service of a body of night telephonists who have no other employment are engaged for as little as 12 hours per week. If these men on entry are not attending the P.A.C. that is their ultimate destination.

The Post Office surplus hitherto was wholly taken by the Treasury, now a margain is retained by the P.M.G., who may use it for purposes of development only.

Had this been so in the past, the financial position, taking a period from 1892 to 1935, would to-day have been that the Post Office would have had its present equipment and would be free from debt of £110 million which imposes, in addition to the declared surplus, an approximate figure of £9½ million as interest and loan charges on borrowed capital.

This shows that the P.O. provides not only relief for the taxpayer, but gives profit to those taxpayers who happen to have money invested with the Government.

The Executive were twice defeated on the report of the Standing Orders Committee. First on the question of rejected nominations and secondly on the question of the direct Parliamentary Representation Society. The conference refused time for this to be debated.

I have been informed that there are to be private sessions on the wages question and the sorting machines.

The Morning After

IT was a great binge. That can be admitted. The brewers, contemplating the mountains of empty barrels and the bulging cash-tills, will be among the first to agree.

The proprietors of luxury hotels and restaurants, looking over the accounts, will be equally enthusiastic.

It was a blind—a riot. They let themselves go . . . and how. In the West End, fantastic revels. In the dreary purlieus off City Road, beer-parties and dancing, tea-parties for the kiddies, all spread on tables in amazingly decorated streets closed to traffic by the orders of the inhabitants themselves.

Everywhere pubs filled to overflowing. Hundreds of thousands revelling in the opportunity of a glorious day to wash out all anxieties and fears in blessed forgetfulness.

Forgotten the landlord and the boss, the short week and the P.A.C.

And now the morning after.

The grim figures loom up again. The rent man will be on his rounds. The U.A.B. will get busy on the relief scales.

Savings gone. After the short week of Easter, the short week of Jubilee; and nothing in hand for the coming short week of Whitsun. Visits to "uncle" will be frequent. Jubilee Year will be memorable as a record year of short weeks.

Are we saying all these things just for the fun of being nasty?

Certainly not. We know the solace of a binge which blots out cares—and King George's Jubilee is, for the mass of those workers who seized the opportunity, just an opportunity, and little more.

But the point is that not only is there no shadow of the rent man or the Means Test for King George and his class on their morning after;

the question is, what do they hope to gain from this lavish outpouring of the wine of forgetfulness?

'Look at the posters on the hoardings:—

"BEGIN YOUR ARMY CAREER IN JUBILEE YEAR."

That brings back another reminder with a jerk. While the mass binge raises "loyal" enthusiasm, the powers behind the scenes are going on steadily preparing the job for which you, who may follow the recruiting sergeant's appeal, will be required.

Certain armaments works were carrying on yesterday at full blast, regardless of Jubilee.

This Jubilee enthusiasm carries the mind back to the delirious days of 1914, when the arms race reached its inevitable conclusion.

An intoxicated mass is now being exploited by the ruling class to win enthusiastic support for its programme of naval and Air Force extension.

The parallel is ominous. The war to which they are driving provides the working-class with its morning after the slaughter. And them with theirs of profiteering and loot.

reign of George V. The place was near Leicester Square and there were four of us, one on each corner of an intersection. I call it a sales pitch but such was the interest that all we had to do was hand out the paper and take the money. When there was a pause in business we shouted pre-arranged slogans such as 'Jubilee celebrations are war preparations!' and 'end 15 years of hunger and war!' In less than one hour we sold 50 copies each and had to return to base to collect further supplies which we did not get because other sellers had also sold out.

At this stage I had not met my future husband Roland, whose activities in the party and outside it had earned him the nickname 'Lucky' – which was perhaps why he was chosen for one of the risky jobs on Jubilee day. While I was selling on the street corner he was already watching in the Strand to see if the banner which read 'Long May they Reign' would change into '25 years of Hunger and War' as the Royal Coach containing King George and Queen Mary passed under it. It did and there was quite a cheer for the effort.

Whilst Lucky was one of the 'behind the scenes' people on the job the real hero was a short unemployed painter called Mac who donned a white coat and carried a tool bag. Passing himself off as a workman – 'Mr Grainger of the Ministry of Works' – Mac gained access to the offices where the ropes for the banner were situated and with the help of another comrade in an office the other side of the road 'doctored' the banner to bring about the transformation.

The demonstration at the Jubilee Celebrations was part of the Party's campaign against the private manufacture and sales of armaments which culminated in the Royal Commission on the Private Manufacture of and Trading in Arms. Harry Pollit, General Secretary of the Communist Party, gave evidence both in writing and verbally to the Commission. His evidence alleged that the United Kingdom was the main centre of the world's armament trade and was responsible for about one-third of all arms exports. It also pointed out that in the 1914–18 war some 800,000 British troops were killed and two million were wounded, some by British arms, notably in the Dardanelles.

Living in Bloomsbury was, to me, like living in the centre of the world and I was free to take advantage of it. I was free to go where I wanted to, to have friends in when I felt like it, see the sights of the city, and even take a trip down the river. For some months I did very few of these things because I soon realised I was also free to be lonely. I kept on with my writing and with my learning through reading. I became more and more convinced that the system of private enterprise and private profit underpinned by sharp competition was not only morally wrong but was wasteful, cruel, unfair, caused a great deal of human unhappiness and ultimately led to destruction.

Among my brother's friends I found plenty of people to agree with me, students who were organised in student political societies and were active in the political scene. I learned from them how to express myself on political matters but I did not learn how to take some action. They acted through their student bodies. I had to look for something else.

My search for something else was spurred on by my realisation that to be sympathetic to the lot of the unemployed and to blame the system which exploited them without making some sort of protest was not only non-productive but also hypocritical. In my middle-class way of life, living on an allowance of four pounds a week – twice the average wage for workers in industry – I could do little, or so I thought, but at least I could protest.

Again I turned to my younger brother for advice. He was clear in his mind. We must join the Communist Party because it was the only party which was actually doing anything. We did consider joining the Labour Party but it seemed much too milk-and-water. At least the Communist Party proclaimed there would be a bitter fight for a better future and had a theoretical basis for its actions.

The decision was somewhat difficult for me. I was a pacifist and the policy of the Communist Party, while it was against war, was anything but pacifist. I joined anyway, juggling with my conscience, which was not very strong and coming down on the side of joining. The reason I did not hold back was partly because had I done so I would have been isolated from my brother and his friends at LSE, the only friends I had at the time.

Perhaps subconsciously I joined the party to give me a base, to give my life a structure, to give me a reason for getting up in the morning. I had already realised that London was the loneliest place I had ever been in. Everyone was so busy while I had a vast amount of time and nothing to do. Not having a job in Southport where I was surrounded by family and friends was one thing. Not having a job in a strange city was another cup of tea. To fill my time I tried writing again. Writing involved thinking and my thoughts turned to weighing up whether I was really better off in London on my own. Life in Southport did have its brighter moments. I'd become quite a good golf player and won prizes at the local club where my father was the captain, and I got acquainted with top players such as Harry and Arnold Bentley and even Henry Cotton when the big tournaments were held at my father's club. I even played with Henry Cotton – Henry, Harry Bentley, my sister Joyce and I occasionally played a foursome. Was living in London compensation for three square meals a day, regular paid visits to the theatre and cinema, dances, parties, trips to the races including the Grand National which was virtually on our doorstep, and other socially useless pursuits?

I finally decided that I should stick it out. As I became more involved in the activities of the Holborn branch of the Communist Party, I had more commitments, more friends and I was learning all the time.

THE FIRST NATIONAL

Children's Rights Conference

MARY WARD HALL   LONDON   WC1
SATURDAY AND SUNDAY MARCH 11 & 12
(Saturday 10-5 pm, 6.30-9pm; Sunday 10.30-4pm)

Roland Berger, Political Stunts

(transcribed by Vicki Berger from his written anecdotes)

AN AMUSING PERIOD IN MY LIFE was in the early nineteen-thirties when with several kindred spirits, Claude Cockburn, Philip Jordan, Philip Harding, we formed ourselves into a loosely knit group, associated also loosely with the Agit Prop department of the CP. Alec Anderson, friend of Howard Coster, the photographer, was indirectly attached, more on the public relations side. Our operations grew out of the need to get publicity for the opposition to Oswald Mosely and his fascists. A rally had been called by the Fascists in Hyde Park and Harry Pollitt (General Secretary of the CP) had given the call 'Drown them in a sea of working class activity.' But the media played the whole thing down suggesting that the best answer to the Fascists was to laugh at them. Pollitt and the Agit Prop department posed the question 'How to break through the media blanket.'(We cogitated. With some help from a friend in the BBC we) (deleted by RB) Selecting a restaurant in the Strand, Romanos, which had an evening Dinner Dansant which was broadcast, we prepared two comrades, a man and a woman, suitably dressed, evening dress for the man and a gown for the girl, to dine and dance. At some stage of the evening, the girl approaches the bandleader to ask for a specific number. Whilst his attention is engaged the man picks up the microphone and makes a call for everyone to come to Hyde Park to oppose the Fascists. Interviewed by the representatives of the BBC the man explains that he is unemployed and that in this one evening his meal had cost as much as his benefit for the week.

An ingenious stunt I organised was to rouse attention to the imprisonment of Ernst Thälmann by the Nazis. From friends in the film business we got news that the projection room at the London Pavilion Cinema was, illegally, left unlocked and the cleaners who went in, in the early morning, left the outer door unlocked. We had a short length of film prepared with 'Release Thälmann, Down with Fascism' inserted. We then had to decide when to do the deed to be seen by the greatest number of people. On a weekday only a dribble of audience could be present. So we decided upon a Saturday. Four of our people slipped in .....[illegible] a film from the can, cut it and then inserted our piece. The film was Walt Disney's *Peculiar Penguins*. I went down to the cinema to see what happened. After the Certificate 'Approved by the British Board of Film Censors', the film opened with music and a few odd penguins strutting over the ice. Then a blackout and 'Release Thälmann,' in bold letters on the screen. After a ....[illegible], I slipped out of the cinema and telephoned the cinema in the name of the Associated Press. I had been told that a slogan appeared on the screen. What had the manager to say? He denied any such thing, scared, apparently that he would be prosecuted for breaking the fire regulations. I then phoned the Press with the story, who incidentally asked if I had a contact for the information. It seems that the cinema was unaware of the method we had used, assumed that the slogan had been flashed from the body of the cinema and had run the film a second time.

Not long after, we organised a stunt at the German Embassy in the Mall. Discovering that the house next door was empty we arranged for one of our friends (Winchester & Balliol) to call the estate agents and arrange to view. He took along one of our friends, ostensibly a builder. After a preliminary chit-chat, he suggested to the estate agent that his builder would like to have a look at the roof. Once on the roof our mate hoisted a flag 'Release Thälmann.' The last, the most imaginative, and the most daring was conceived, masterminded and organised by myself on the occasion of George V's Jubilee (6 May 1935). This was the test case, when we had to rise to the occasion. It started by my going over the site. Walking down Fleet Street, near Ludgate Circus I saw the opportunity. I had conceived an idea – a banner – the inner part fixed on a wire and outside two flaps held by a string running through curtain rings. When the string was pulled away the two flaps dropped to reveal our slogans on the outside. The banner said 'Long May he Reign'. On the flaps was written '20 years of Hunger & War' and 'Long Live the Communist International.' But how to arrange? My inspection of the route revealed the possible sites: on the left the *Birmingham Post* and on the right the *Irish Independent*. The banner would be stretched between the two. On the right side alongside the *Irish Independent* ran a little ginnel leading to a church. This would provide the best place for the string to be placed to release the flap.

SECRET.

To THE POSTMASTER-GENERAL, and all others whom it may concern :

    I hereby authorize and require you to detain, open and produce for my inspection all postal packets and telegrams addressed to :—

> Roland BERGER and Nancy BERGER,
> 5 Grove Terrace,
> Highgate Road,
> LONDON, N.W.5.

or to any name at that or any other address if there is reasonable ground to believe that they are intended for the said   Roland BERGER and Nancy BERGER

and for so doing this shall be your sufficient Warrant.

These persons are prominent Communists. She has been a member of the Communist Party since 1936 and is known to engage in secret work on behalf of the Party Headquarters. It is desired to investigate her contacts and activities, and those of her husband, more fully.

> *One of Her Majesty's*
> *Principal Secretaries of State.*

S. Form 56.

PF. 52673/F.1.A.

VI
Life in the Communist Party

Nancy WHITTAKER
SBSH report dated 3.3.37

WHITTAKER has a flat at 36 Clare Court, Judd Street, WC The flat is a fairly expensive one, but is in her Mother's name; her Mather live in London, at another address, but frequently visits her daughter. WHITTAKER is known to SSBSH as a member of the National Council for Civil Liberties, but otherwise has not come to the notice of SB. She is a friend of well-known communists, and does not appear to have any regular work. She is about 22 years old, 5'4" in heaight,[sic] very light brown hair parted on one side, fresh complexion. Usually dressed in tweeds and hatless.

Nancie Whittaker From Metropolitan Police   30/6/38.
Special Branch

Nancie Whittaker does most of the editorial work of the Holborn Outlook at her home address at 36 Clare Court, Judd Street, W.C.1>. She is visited at her home address by seral young persons of the communist type, and Birt is known to her. She is mentioned in S.B. file 320/SE/697, report dated 27/1/38 as being a member of a communist group which formerly had its headquarters at 40 Coram St. W.C.1. Her brother, Peter Hon [sic] Whittaker, also mentioned in that report, is believed to be still in Spain.

Copy of report from C.C. Southport, dated 13.7.39.

Dear Sir Vernon Kell,

With reference to your letter of the 11th May, No. PF.47461/B.4a.
I have to inform you that Peter, Joyce, and Nancy Whittaker are the
children of Schofield Whittaker, Cotton Waste Merchant, of 69 Albert
Road, Southport.

These three children have been a continual source of worry to
their farther owing to their extremist views. Peter and Joyce are known
personally to Detective Inspector Mighall of this Force, but Nancy is the
most determined and extreme in her views, and she is likely to be the
Secretary of the local branch of the Communist Party. She approached me
when the Trades' Union Congress were meeting at Southport a few weeks
ago, for permission ot use an ambulance which had been return from Spain
to make collections on the streets for Chinese refugees. Her request was
not acceded to.

For years these young people have not been compelled to consider
their future owing to the over-indulgence of their father, and it is likely that
they would drop a number of their pursuits in the event of his death.

I attach hereto a cutting from the Southport Visiter, dated the 20th
May, 1939, giving details of the recent activities of these young people,
together with photographs of Peter and Joyce Whittaker, which may be
of interest.

Much of the attitude of these persons is regarded as pose, but we
have taken a considerable interest in them for some time and will continue
to keep them under observation. They have never attempted to conceal
their opinions and sympathies.

Yours sincerely,

Sgd: M.J. Egan
Major, Chief Constable

I REMEMBER THE DAY we joined the Party.
It was at an open meeting of the Holborn branch at a hall in central
London, probably the Conway Hall. I think we imagined we were going
to be welcomed with open arms and have the red carpet laid down for us.
It was not quite like that. We signed on the dotted line and paid our first
month's dues. We were told that our first task would be selling the *Daily
Worker* at an early morning pitch outside a Tube station. That and
attendance at the meeting of the branch once a month would be all the
commitments we would take on for the present. There were no welcoming
noises, no smiles, rather a sullen acceptance that alas the Party had to
have middle class people in it even if they were pretty useless. So, we
went off to the cinema feeling that joining the Party was not such a big
deal after all.

My acceptance into the Party branch was equally lukewarm. Even
though the branch was in an area filled with the middle class and intellectuals, the comrades in the branch were mainly working class who looked
upon the rest of the population as a spineless mass backing up the ruling
class, protesting now and again in order to retain a progressive image.
As a member of this mass I was tolerated – just – and came to realise that,
by virtue of their upbringing and experience, the working class knew what
line to take in opposing the ruling class and furthering the cause of the
revolution. People like myself had to think hard about what action was
correct and study deeply before they could hope to take the right line
and even understand the line taken by others.

Things got better as I got more involved in Party work. The man who
had admitted me was a street sweeper called John who thought the middle
class were all a load of shits but other members of the branch were more

sympathetic. Before I knew where I was, I was up to my eyeballs in leafleting, selling the *Daily Worker*, stewarding meetings, attending demonstrations, and heaven knows what else. My brother Peter had been transferred to the branch at the London School of Economics where he was a student. I felt very lost without his support partly because I was much less well read than he was and partly because I did not agree with the Party line anyway and he was the only one I could discuss this huge dilemma with. I was still a pacifist and remained so until future events changed my mind: my brother joined the International Brigades and was soon at the front.

In spite of everything I threw myself into Party work with a great deal of enthusiasm and a lot of efficiency. The latter was not always appreciated by comrades who saw orderly organisation as bourgeois. But for the most part my middle-class abilities were accepted as necessary. I was made education secretary and told to get on with setting up training classes. It was probably the luckiest 'appointment' I ever had since it marked the beginning of my own education in Marxism, an education which went on all my life and compensated me for the poor education I got at my day and boarding schools.

One of the main activities of the Holborn branch was Marxist education. At least once a week there would be a lecture followed by discussion and because of the location of the branch, in the centre of the university area, the branch was able to draw on some of the best brains in the Party to give lectures. So, one heard Pat Sloan, Douglas Garman, John Mahon, Robin Jardine, Hubert Nicholson, Robin and Olive Arnot, John Lewis, and Margaret Mynatt, to mention only a few. Not all of the 'intellectuals' in the Party were 'open' members and this fact led to my first contretemps with the branch.

Getting people to give lectures was easier than getting people to listen to them. Nevertheless, my first organising effort as education secretary was a great success: a large percentage of the branch attended; the list of lectures I had pasted up on the wall of the Party rooms was much read and I could see people noting in their diaries the days of the lectures. I was quite pleased with myself. My elation did not last long. I was summoned to the house of the Party secretary. When I arrived, I was confronted by Edith Bone, a Hungarian refugee and long-time member of the Hungarian Communist Party, based in Moscow, lying on a divan, dressed in a blue Burberry type mackintosh and a blue beret. I was not invited to sit down. Edith Bone started her interrogation the moment I arrived. Did I not realise that I was endangering the livelihood of one of our comrades? I had absolutely no idea what she was talking about. Did I not know that

THE PUBLIC ORDER ACT, 1936

East End Disturbances.

When Sir Oswald Mosley, in September, 1936, announced his intention of marching his uniformed anti-Jewish force through the Jewish quarter of London, it was not seriously disputed that his action would lead to very serious breaches of the peace. As is pointed out in the article on "Anti-Semitism in East London" on page 1. Members of Parliament had warned Sir John Simon and the Government, on March 5th and July 10th, that there would be serious riots and bloodshed in the East End if the police did not take energetic steps to check the provocation and Jew-baiting in which the Fascists had so long been indulging. After these serious warnings in the House of Commons, the culminating point was reached with Sir Oswald Mosley's provocative announcement of a march which, by its very nature, must result in breaches of the peace. There were immediate protests from responsible persons in East London and an influentially-signed petition containing some thousands of signatures was presented to the Home Secretary begging him to use his powers to prevent this threatened action by the Fascists.

In view of the high feeling which existed in the East End, Mayors and Councillors of East End Boroughs went on a deputation to the Home Secretary. Sir John Simon, when he received the deputation, led them to believe that he could not intervene. What he did not tell these municipal officials was the fact that for practically a hundred years the police have had the power to *regulate the routes of processions* under the Metropolitan Police Act, 1839, and in provincial centres under the Town Police Clauses Acts.

If Sir John Simon argued that he himself was not the official charged with the duty of preventing this provocative uniformed march from entering an area where it would cause serious trouble, he might well have informed his listeners that a word from him to the Commissioner of Police of the Metropolis would be sufficient to cause Sir Philip Game to exercise his powers under the Metropolitan Police Act and forbid the Fascist procession to march through the Jewish quarter. Sir Philip did in fact exercise these powers on Sunday, October 4th, an hour or more after serious rioting had broken out, and we may well ask why he failed in his duty of taking action in advance to prevent these riots breaking out rather than allowing the trouble to develop before exercising his powers. When he exercised them he insisted that the Blackshirts should go West and not East, and the Blackshirt procession ultimately took place along the Embankment, where it disbanded.

The police have always possessed the power of taking preventive action against any person who threatens some course of action which is likely to lead to a breach of the law. The police, therefore, had they wished to do so, could have issued a summons before the march, requiring Sir Oswald Mosley to appear before a magistrate to show cause why he should not be bound over to be of good behaviour and to keep the peace when he was threatening so serious a disturbance of the peace.

Police chiefs, both in London and the provinces, have repeatedly interfered with Labour and other processions, even within the last few months. They invariably regulate the routes of processions such as May Day demonstrations, which are held every year, and already, as we go to Press, the Commissioner has intimated to the First of May Committee that he proposes to exercise his powers under the Metropolitan Police Act by diverting the May Day procession this year from what he considers an unsuitable route. In 1932, Mr. Tom Mann was the nominal head of the Hunger Marchers, and in that year, before the arrival of the marchers in London, he was summoned to appear at Bow Street and was ordered to be bound over to be of good behaviour and keep the peace. Why then did Sir John Simon not inform the Mayors and Councillors of the East End Boroughs that the police would take similar action against Sir Oswald Mosley? If Mr. Tom Mann, in circumstances far less critical than those which existed in October last, could be ordered to be bound over, why could not the leader of the Blackshirt semi-military force, carrying its anti-Semitic campaign into the heart of the Jewish quarter, have been similarly bound over, and the October disturbances have been thus avoided?

some comrades had to operate 'underground' because if they came out into the open they would lose their jobs? I did not know that either. I was about to ask what this one-sided conversation was all about when Edith Bone sat bolt upright and yelled 'You have jeopardised a man's job. Don't you realise this?' I thought for a moment and the answer was still no. Edith Bone was becoming quite frantic. In other countries, such actions would be punishable by death – a shot in the head. By this time, I was not only very confused but also very frightened. I asked Edith Bone to explain exactly what I had done. Amid a lot of abuse, I gathered that my crime was to have included a man's name in the list of lecturers I had pasted on the wall of the Party rooms. He was a sub-editor on a Sunday newspaper and as such vulnerable. If his employers found out he was a Party member he would almost certainly be sacked.

I apologised as best I could, but it was not accepted. I wondered if I ought to tender my resignation to the Party and suggested this. Edith Bone flew into another tantrum. I would not be allowed to resign, she said, but I might be expelled. As things stood I would probably be allowed to remain in the branch provided I worked hard. I left the room wondering why it was Edith Bone who reprimanded me and not the branch secretary. It was years before I found out that Edith was an old 'Party lag' who meddled wherever she could. Years later, after the war, when she went back to Hungary, she was jailed as a spy. Later still she was released and turned up in my NUJ branch. I did not remind her of our previous encounter.

My membership of the Communist Party was very important to me. Just how important was not clear at the time but as I learned more and studied enough to call myself a Marxist I realised that it had virtually changed my life. On the most superficial level it provided me with human contact of a meaningful nature. On a deeper level, it gave me a sense of history so that I viewed things in longer terms, preventing myself from getting panic stricken when something went wrong or when the world was subjected to some disaster.

Perhaps most important, looking at the picture in broad terms, I was getting an education through the Party. What bit of post-school education I had picked up was through reading at the local public library. Party education gave me a new dimension, a new purpose in life. It was very academic, the sort of learning I had not encountered at school. I struggled with the reading of Marx, Lenin, Engels, and Stalin and probably under-stood less than the working-class comrades who studied with me.

Study was greatly helped by the publications of the Left Book Club founded in 1936 by Victor Gollancz. This book club not only sold books and published *Left Book Club News* – a publication more about politics than about books – but also organised discussion groups on a large scale. There was a main choice of book each month and also a series of extra items which one could purchase. All were at low prices and many of us built up libraries from purchases through this club. All the books were written from a Marxist point of view, and while they dealt with complex subjects such as the relationships between Freud and Marx they did so in a clear, uncomplicated manner.

The Left Book Club provided me with my first paid job in London: a straightforward clerical job. In a top room in Henrietta Street I sorted club members' address cards into some sort of regional order. There seemed to be thousands of them and indeed there were thousands of members of the club. It was formed at a time of high political awareness and people were eager for knowledge.

The job provided me with a bit of cash to supplement the allowance my father was giving me and also some work experience which I needed badly. It was all part of the 'left' world I had entered and in which I continued to live, in one form or another, for the rest of my life.

Looking back, I wonder what would have happened to me had I not joined the Party and I shudder when I conjure up a middle-class woman with nothing much in her head or her life. The 1931 Wall Street crash had produced massive unemployment, and this, the war in Spain, the fight against fascism, cuts in already inadequate wages and benefits were the issues on which the Party was running campaigns. Perhaps most prominent and perhaps most effective in bringing people together was the campaign to persuade the Western allies to provide the democratically elected government of Spain with the opportunity to buy arms. Instead, Britain and France carried out a pious, hypocritical policy of so-called non-intervention. On the other side the Germans and the Italians were supplying arms to Franco without restriction. On the domestic front the passing of the Public Order Act, 1936, which was ostensibly to stop uniformed organisations demonstrating and which gave the police wide powers to stop demonstrations of all kinds, caused difficulties for the left-wing organisations because the police used their wide powers to stop demonstrations by the left.

The campaign against the Public Order Act was carried out by the National Council for Civil Liberties formed in 1934 by liberals and others who feared a general onslaught on the freedom of the individual.

It was the war in Spain which affected me most. I had joined the Party with very definite pacifist leanings but the war in Spain had caused me to think very carefully about this position. When my brother Peter announced that he had joined the International Brigades and was leaving for Paris in two days' time, my feelings quickly started to change into an almost violent aggression against fascism. In the following months whenever I went on demonstrations calling for arms to be sent to Spain in order that the properly elected government could fight the fascists, I would be out of line in a flash if anyone challenged us, shouting abuse and telling them of my brother's involvement. It was over the course of this war that the practical events and demonstrations changed my attitude from that of pacifism to the use of violence in the cause of revolution.

Peter's departure for Spain was full of complications. The whole operation, from London to Paris and then transit to Spain, had to be kept secret so only a few close friends were told. Breaking the news to our parents was more difficult, as we assumed that they would be opposed to the whole venture not only on the grounds of the hazards of war but also on political grounds, either in opposition to the legally elected government, or through lack of knowledge and understanding about the situation.

Our first ploy was to say that Peter had gone to drive an ambulance, thinking this was more acceptable than actual fighting, so a letter was sent from Paris to this effect. Sitting at home waiting for the news to break was my sister Joyce, who was in on the plot and pretending to know nothing about it. The explosion was not quite as dramatic as we had imagined it would be. My mother cried but soon recovered and later even told her friends the news with some pride. My father, however, raged and decided to claim that my brother was 'having an affair in Paris'. The whole pretence became too complicated to sustain so my brother finally wrote to my father telling him he had joined the International Brigades as a soldier and not as an ambulance driver.

The effect of this letter was electric but not in the way we expected. On 2 March 1938 Peter wrote to me saying that he had received a letter from my father. It had read, 'Surprised. Yes! I did not think I had anything to do with this job. At least I didn't think so as I didn't even read the news or look at the pictures but just felt sorry for the whole lot. Now I have got a 'side'. I hope you are keeping alright and soon will be able to give us some news about yourself and the sooner we get you back the better. Let me know whatever you may require and we will send it. God bless you and look after yourself. Your loving father. PS Play up our side.' Peter's comment was, 'Pretty good, eh? What price the PS?' My mother wrote that she and father were reconciled to Peter's action and 'regard it as something to be proud of'.

For us at home, these letters were like the lifting of a prison sentence. It meant the end of the deceit and the start of trying to get mother and father involved in the campaign of aid for Spain. My mother joined my sister Joyce in collecting money, organising meetings and sending off food to Spain. My father could not quite bring himself to take part in politics aside from sending cash to Peter. Joyce's contribution, at this time, was quite major. In a town like Southport there were not too many people sympathetic to the Republican cause, nevertheless Joyce's efforts resulted in hundreds of people being involved and donating food and cash for medical aid. She brought many well-known speakers – I can remember the former Labour MP and Communist Party theorist John Strachey, and George Jegar, the Mayor of Shoreditch and Organising-Secretary of the Spanish Medical Aid Committee, both visiting.

It must have been very difficult for my mother and father to support the cause of the Spanish government. All their friends and acquaintances would have been against it and in fact most of them would believe, as a great many people in Britain believed, that the rightful Spanish government was Franco's and that the war had been started by the Communists. It was hard to convince people who were not politically minded that the government had been democratically elected.

To a considerable section of the British establishment Franco was carrying out a necessary crusade against communism. This section had as its 'front' the Catholic Church, the *Daily Mail* owned by Lord Rothermere, which had at the time the third largest circulation of any newspaper, the *Daily Sketch*, the *Morning Post*, and the *Observer*.

The rest of the press were, in a half-hearted way, against Franco but made no attempt to tell their readers the true position about non-interventions. Only the *News Chronicle* and the *Daily Worker* did this, both demanding that the right of the Spanish republican government to buy arms be honoured. Throughout the war only the Soviet Union supplied the government with arms.

Looking back, it is remarkable that a government which, when elected in 1933, did not contain any communists and or any socialists was represented in this way. It was only after the elections in January 1936 and in the reorganisation of the government in September that year, twenty -two months after the initial success of the republicans and a couple of months after the fascist rebellion, that the left socialist, Caballero, was made Prime Minister and invited communists to serve as ministers in his government.

In addition to those who supported the Republican Government against the fascists because they saw the long term political repercussions of its defeat there were those who gave their support because they heeded one of the principles of international socialism: the support of the weak against the strong. It is hard today to appreciate how strong this feeling was, especially among the working class who because they were the underdogs themselves gave their support to action by the underdogs of the world.

Those of us who spent our evenings and sometimes our nights distributing leaflets, speaking at meetings and demonstrations, and generally spreading information about the conflict in Spain believed that left to themselves the Spanish people would defeat the fascist rebels. It was not in our thinking that the people would be defeated by a military coup although we realised it was going to be a tough struggle and the Spanish people would need the support of the democratic sections of the world. What we had not reckoned on was the enormous amount of help in the form of arms and manpower that the fascist powers of Italy and Germany were giving to Franco. German planes ferried Moorish troops from Africa into Southern Spain and supplies of weapons, ammunition, and troops from both countries flooded into the fighting areas.

Approaches to the French government to allow the Republican government to buy arms in accordance with existing trade agreements were refused. At first Blum, then Prime Minister of France, agreed but later, after pressure from the British government, he changed his mind and agreed to a policy of non-intervention. This was announced as 'putting both sides in the conflict on the same basis' which was a surprising concept since existing international practice was to help the established government rather than a rebelling section of the population.

The members of the non-intervention committee included Germany and Italy but they continued to pour arms into Spain. At first the USSR was a member but later withdrew when it became increasingly clear that the two fascist powers were not going to stop supporting the rebels. From then on, the elected government of Spain could buy arms from the Soviet Union but transportation difficulties limited the amount.

Letters from my brother from the front to which he had been transferred after a few weeks of training spoke of hanging about doing nothing very much, explanations of why he could not tell us anything positive, and urging us to write often, not about the general news because they got copies of the *Daily Worker* at the front, but about gossipy items of everyday occurrence. 'These make good reading here,' he wrote. 'This sort of news – about what you are all doing – makes me feel better. I realise then that there is something to come home to. The feeling that one may never come home is very strange. News of what is going on helps me to believe that I will survive.'

In early March 1938 Peter wrote that he had been made Company

Secretary and was now on Company Headquarters staff, 'Not because of any special merit but because of general intelligence,' he wrote. 'It's rather pleasant though, as when one is not in action one gets very introspective and depressed but when you have a special job there is something to do all the time.'

Later he wrote, 'Now, about action. As I said in my previous letter I can't say much about it yet. You will have got the general idea of it from the papers – colossal offensive by the fascists and retreat by us. The only reason that made it possible was Franco's avion and artillery – one just could not stay there and remain alive. But I won't say more or this letter will be stopped.

'After I had been in Spain a short time I felt a changed person but now I feel as though I have changed even more. It makes one really understand how terribly important and serious politics are. It has made me really understand for the first time the meaning of the old Marxist tag the fusing of Theory and Practice. To have talked about Spain and war for so long and then actually experiencing the situation is very curious. It makes one realise how many irresponsible things we have said about the situation here and the stupid doubt one had as to the correctness of the line.

'Of course that is absolutely inexcusable when one is not actually in the thing itself but it certainly makes us more careful when discussing other things. As to my opinion of war I can do no better than repeat the title of some book or other *War is Hell*, and if I ever hear anyone say (as I have often said when feeling bored or hoping to see a Marxist analysis proved correct) that they wish a war would start I would probably shoot them.

'I don't think I was as frightened when fighting as I thought I would be. It is surprising how indifferent to bullets one becomes. The only thing which really scares me is the ground strafing by avion, but the worst thing about this action (which old timers say was worse than anything they'd seen including Brunete, etc.) was the suspense, as one was never sure as to whether one was surrounded or not.*

'Finally, although I expect the papers are saying the thing is practically finished, I honestly think that we shall fix the bastards yet – that is if we can get the arms and artillery.'

The end was nearer than he thought. A few weeks later he was in a Franco jail. The members of his company had been, so they thought, advancing to a new position to the east of Alcañiz on the Aragon front

* The Battle of Brunete (6–25 July 1937), fought fifteen miles west of Madrid, was a Republican attempt to alleviate the pressure exerted by the Nationalists on the capital and on the north during the Spanish Civil War. Initially successful, the Republicans were forced to retreat from Brunete and suffered devastating casualties from the battle.

BRITISH PRISONERS RELEASED BY THE SPANISH INSURGENTS

It was reported on October 26 that twenty more British prisoners released by the Spanish Insurgents had crossed the international bridge at Hendaye, 80 of the 100 men whom the Insurgents were releasing having left Spain. The photograph shows some of the British prisoners marching into France. Twenty prisoners had previously crossed the ~~~~ on Tuesday of last week. A party who had been released earlier landed at Newhaven from France on October 25.

when they were ordered to stop and fall out on the side of the road to wait for a mechanised column to pick them up. The volunteers sat listening to the roar of tanks as they approached. To their astonishment the tanks were Franco's, manned by Italians who roared with laughter at the consternation of the British volunteers.

Before he was captured, Peter's letters gave a heartening description of the organisation of the army and behind the lines. As he travelled through Spain in a train he said life was going on much as it always did and apart from a chronic shortage of food the population was not too badly off except in places which were being constantly bombed. When the trains stopped at small stations children would offer oranges in exchange for bread and tobacco.

'I am afraid my perspective has become extremely narrow, due I suppose because of the new situation but partly because of the lack of news. I reckon it is easier to study the position in Spain from England than it is from the front,' he wrote.

The lack of letters from home, the shortage of cigarettes, and the monotony of the food were probably the greatest hardships Peter felt at the front.

By September 1938 there were already rumours in Britain and in the jails of an exchange of British prisoners in the hands of Franco for Italian prisoners in the hands of the Republican government. No one among the Brigadiers knew who was to be chosen but with the setting up of a commission to negotiate the exchange, numbers began to be mentioned.

On 4 October 1938 Peter wrote to tell us that a week previously a British agent had visited the camp and told the prisoners that an exchange had definitely been agreed and that Barcelona was to exchange ninety-nine Italian prisoners for ninety-nine British ones. The number had originally been 100 on each side but an Englishman had died during the negotiations. 'The exchange is to be done in batches of twenty,' he wrote, 'and the first batch will be leaving for home in a few days. By the way I've had the luck to be in the first twenty.' He told us that they would travel to St Jean de Luz, near the French–Spanish border, where the British Consul would take charge, probably putting them on the Dieppe–Newhaven ferry. Once on British soil they would be left to their own devices and would see their way home at their own expense. He wrote, 'We were told that the British government would charge us four pounds for this and we have to sign a declaration saying we would be willing to pay this sum.' 'Well, I hope the bastards get it!' he added.

As early as July 1938 I had been in communication with a journalist friend in Vancouver. He had written that Peter would soon be home, he could assure me of this, but the whys and wherefores he could not reveal. 'Never tell anyone of my intervention,' he said in his letter. 'Let anyone take the credit for his release rather than me.' It was all rather cloak and dagger and I have never got to the bottom of it because I lost touch with our journalist friend soon after Peter was released.

From the time we first heard of his possible release we scoured the newspapers and listened to as many newscasts as we could manage. When the news came it was through a picture in the *News Chronicle* of the released prisoners crossing the bridge at Hendaye. There was Peter on the outside column looking well and confident. I rushed round to the flat of James Jeffery, over a fish shop in Marchmont Street which, because of the smell, was not to be visited except at the most urgent moments. He was still in bed and his response was typical. 'Go back to your flat,' he said 'and start cooking a "Sunday" breakfast. I'll be over shortly.'

In a few days Peter and a number of other International Brigadiers arrived at Victoria station. All his old mates were there to meet him as well as a big crowd of supporters of the Republican government. He was a bit blown up by a diet of beans and he had dysentery but otherwise he was reasonably fit.

In September 1938 the Spanish Prime Minister Negrin announced that all foreign volunteers in Spain would be repatriated. It was a last desperate attempt to force the withdrawal of German and Italian soldiers who were fighting on Franco's side. At this time my brother reported that 250,000 Italian and 50,000 German troops were in Spain.

On 7 December 1938 the remaining 300-odd International Brigadiers returned home arriving at Victoria Station where around 20,000 people welcomed them.

By the end of January 1939 Barcelona had fallen. In March the much-bombed Madrid surrendered.

Life without my brother Peter had been difficult. The contact I'd had with his friends at LSE had fallen away and for the most part I was left with only the comrades in the Communist Party branch who, at this juncture, were somewhat alien to me. I had not adjusted to being friendly with working-class people whose social and personal habits were so different from my own. Their idea of a night out for example was a bit of a blowout in the pub. Mine was a night at the theatre or cinema, both of which seemed a waste of time to my new comrades. The one good friend Peter had made at LSE was James Jeffreys, a postgraduate student of some brilliance who was the main speaker for the Communist branch in LSE. He was not exactly someone in whom one could confide but he was, more or less, on my wavelength, and on many occasions when I was lonely he came to the rescue with a visit to the cinema. Born in South London James had been brought up in the most suburban types of London home. He had to some extent opted out of social contact early in his life and cut himself off from small talk and social graces long before he went to LSE. I remember a time when my brother took him to stay with our parents in Southport. After his first day my mother asked James what he thought of the place. 'I find it odd,' said James, 'because there are so few working-class people here.' One of the advantages of the area, New Moston near Manchester, to which we had moved to better ourselves, was just the fact that there was no obvious working class – none of the groups of unem-ployed men playing cards, talking or just sitting that had troubled my father. To my mother this answer seemed odd, to say the least. My parents did not take to James. He was too taciturn, too intellectual, too brusque. Nevertheless I think they were proud that their son could claim as a best friend a man who had gained a first in his first degree, written a PhD, and won a Leverhulme Scholarship to the United States. The influence of James on both Peter and myself was considerable. He was the epitome of the lower middle-class lad who had made himself into an intellectual. He passed on to us – perhaps unknowingly – his organised methods of thought, complementary, for me anyway, to the teaching I was getting in the local Party branch. What we tried to teach him, but failed miserably, was that families were important and the support they could give was vital, especially in a crisis.

One of the big disappointments for Peter when he got home from Spain was that James had already left to take up his Leverhulme Scholarship in Harvard, leaving soon after I'd visited him. Since I knew that Peter would need a holiday of some kind I made an agreement with my father to pay half my fare to the States and my expenses there, pro-vided I could raise the other half. We had decided that Peter, his girlfriend Kate, her sister Margot who was James's girlfriend, and myself should leave for New York as soon as possible.

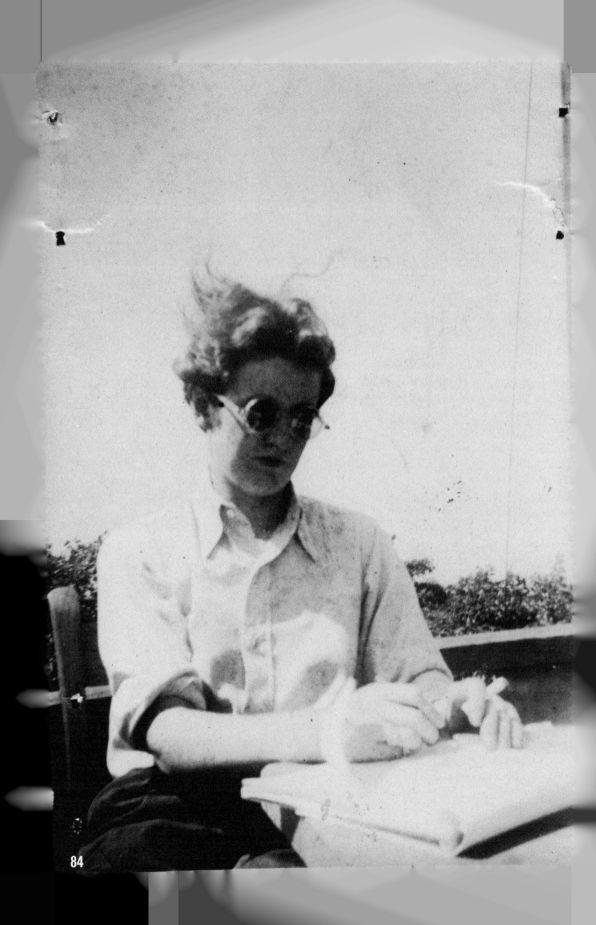

VII
Life in
the USA

WOMAN
FANCY
OR
FREE ?

Delegate to New York Conference

Today Miss Nancy Whittaker, daughter of Mr. and Mrs. Schofield Whittaker, of 69, Albert-road, Southport, sails for New York, where she is to attend a conference. She is one of the official English delegates to the American Writers' League Conference from the Association of Writers of Intellectual Liberty, the other delegates from this country being W. H. Auden, Christopher Isherwood, Ralph Bates and Sylvia Townsend Warner. Miss Whittaker, who will be away about four months, has been in London for some time studying and writing, and though her visit to the States will also be a kind of holiday it will also serve other purposes.

Book and Play

At the present time a book which Miss Whittaker has written is in the hands of the publishers. She is also interested in the theatre, and while in the States will also study the Federal theatre movement, and hopes to get copy for a play which she intends writing in the near future.

May 20th 1939

A TRAVELLING FAMILY

The **Whittaker** sisters, **Joyce** and **Nancy**, of Albert-road and their brother, **Peter** are all due for some travelling during the next few months.

Nancy sailed on Thursday for New York to attend the American Writers' League Conference as an official English delegate from the Association of Writers of Intellectual Liberty, and will be away for about four months. She has been writing in London for some time past, and has just completed a book which is in the publishers' hands.

Her brother Peter, who recently returned from Spain where he had been fighting for the Government, and where he spent several months in a concentration camp as Franco's prisoner, is to join her in New York next month. He is at present studying at London University.

MR. PETER WHITTAKER

Joyce leaves in July for Russia, where she hopes to spend several weeks visiting Leningrad and Moscow, amongst other places, and studying conditions in the Soviet Union. She is a keen Left worker and has been responsible for bringing many famous speakers to Southport in that connexion.

BOAT WAS THE ONLY way of going to the States in 1939 and for those who suffer from seasickness it was a real deterrent. I left first and so suffered my seasickness without smart quips from the others and managed to retain some dignity. James came to New York to meet me, and I found that America had changed him a great deal. He actually said he was very pleased to see me, not at all a James-like remark. Contact with a new kind of people had mellowed him and he was no longer the gruff gawky boy who left Britain only six months before.

My first job in the States was to attend the Congress of the League of American Writers, though this was less a job and rather a commitment to attend and make contact with any US writers who might be willing to write school text books. In England, I was the secretary of a sub-committee of Writers for Intellectual Liberty, a body dominated largely by Annabel Williams-Ellis who felt that writers should pay attention to school books – as many of those in use in schools were so bad. She had recruited on to a committee Rosamund Lehman, Cecil Day-Lewis, Goronwy Rees, and Edmund Penning-Rowsell, who was a publisher. Although the proposition that well known authors should write school books was not very popular with the writers themselves, Annabel did have some success in persuading one or two of them to have a go, and had it not been for the outbreak of the Second World War the idea might have caught on and children would have benefitted.

To give the flavour of the Congress as I tasted it then, I reproduce the material as I wrote it at the time.

Donald Ogden Stewart, a Hollywood script writer, opened the Congress as President (1939). He is one of the men who is responsible for the recent inclination of films towards serious and social themes, and he sounded the keynote of the conference when he said, 'In the beginning there was the word. I quote from a book which is constantly at my bedside (when I am in a hotel) and in the end there will be the word.'

Perhaps the greatest difference between this Congress and the last one, held in 1937, is the emphasis on craft problems. Anyone who has read the published speeches of that year's meetings will know that they could have been made by almost any anti-fascist intellectual whereas the speeches made this year could only have been made by writers. This does not mean that the tenor was any less anti-fascist. Far from it. American writers are acutely conscious that Ivory Towerism means stagnation and they know too that once one comes from the tower anti-fascism is bound to be necessary to any writer who wants to be truthful.

The Congress was divided into craft sessions, an indication that it never looked like being a public political propaganda meeting. Of the eight sessions – Poetry, Literary Criticism, Folk Literature, Drama, Fiction, Radio Writing, Screen Writing, Writers in Exile – I attended all but two. Add to these an opening session where delegates from all over the world reported on a year's progress, a public meeting in Carnegie Hall, and a session devoted to business problems of writers, and you have some idea of the ground covered by 500 delegates sweltering in the New School for Social Research with the temperature well over eighty in the shade.

Almost every well-known writer is a member of the League of American Writers, and many of them were present, speaking at one or other of the sessions. Peadar O'Donnell, Sylvia Townsend Warner from England, Langston Hughes, Louis Aragon from France, Vincent Sheean, Heywood Broun, Dorothy Parker, Malcolm Cowley, Granville Hicks, Pietro di Donato, Christina Stead, Richard Wright, Joseph Freeman, Ludwig Renn, to mention some of them. As well as writers there were many radio personalities, and men and women in the film business, notably Joris Ivens who photographed *Spanish Earth* with Hemingway; Paul Strand; Robert Gessner, Professor of Cinema at New York University; Arch Oboler NBC writer-director of plays; H.V. Kaltenborn, radio news reporter; Norman Corwin and William Robson of CBS writers of documentary scripts.

The Chairman of the Drama session was Lillian Hellman author of *The Little Foxes,* one of the few plays to survive the hot weather, and inevitably the discussion was largely around her play, which is about a southern family at the beginning of the century who are ruining their own and their children's lives by money grubbing. Lillian Hellman has not shirked showing a class in all its brutality but she can be, and was, criticised for dating her play 1900 instead of today. Perhaps it may be argued that an attack on the profit system today would not easily get by the 'censor' but on the other hand an audience is apt to say 'such things may happen in 1900 but today (1939) things are different' and consequently the social usefulness of such a play is somewhat reduced.

Lillian Hellman is best known for her *The Children's Hour*, a play originally banned in Britain and put on privately by the Gate Theatre, but which ran for 650 performances in New York. Subsequently it was made into a film entitled *These Three*. At the moment she is working in Hollywood as a script writer and was responsible for *The Dark Angel* and *Dead End,* among others. Since she left Columbia NYC, she has worked as a theatrical agent, play reader, promoter of summer stock companies and script reading. Her first play *Dear Queen* was never produced.

Two other speeches at this session interested me. One by George Sklar, author of *Life and Death of an American* about which I speak later, emphasised how a much broader canvas than the three act peepshow could be developed in the theatre. He drew examples from his own work which uses living newspaper technique, and from the Soviet Russian theatre. Albert Maltz, author of *Private Hicks,* discussed the affirmative play and pointed out that there was a tendency among those playwrights who attempted to write of people in their struggles to show them as miserable and dejected, neglecting the more triumphant and constructive side of the working class movement.

A good point in connection with the Soviet Theatre was made when someone suggested that even this concerned itself with escapist themes, allowing people to get away from themselves. This criticism was answered when a delegate pointed out that on the contrary Soviet people mainly went to the cinema and to the theatre for exultation and rejoicing in their achievements.

The most interesting craft session was Radio Writing. Not only were some of the foremost radio writers on the platform but also many heads of departments from the various networks. Kaltenborn, who digests news for NBC and who did a twenty-four hour a day coverage of the Munich crisis, was Chairman and led a round table discussion on radio technique which was actually broadcast from the Congress hall. Max Wiley, continuity editor for CBS; Arch Oboler; and Evan Roberts, director of Federal Radio Project (WPA) also took part.

With the aid of recordings of their own scripts, writers explained their use of the air. William Robson chose *No Help Wanted* and *G. Men Against Crime* which were broadcast by the BBC this year (1939). He spoke of social experiments as first class radio material as *No Help Wanted* and Norman Corwin, whose *They Fly Through the Air* is a masterpiece of vivid portrayal of the bombing of a civilian population from the air, showed that in such incidents the radio can be as expressive as the screen. Arch Oboler with *The Ugliest Man* demonstrated a technique which I have not heard used on the English radio: the stream of consciousness. He takes a man whose face is so ugly it shocks onlookers and follows his mind through the years until the man is on the point of committing suicide. From the general thoughts of the man over a long period we come to the detailed watching of his mind, which in contrast is extremely effective.

It is interesting to compare the American Radio with the restriction of the BBC. There seems no doubt that English radio programmes are on the whole more varied, better produced, less crude, and generally of a higher standard technically. On the other hand the scope of subject matter which can be dealt with in English is far less wide than here. Alfred Kreymborg, for instance, produced a sketch tracing the whole Munich agreement using animals for the participating countries. (He chose an ape for England). He told the truth about that ghastly September sell out and he was not banned or thrown out of his job as he might have been in England. Of course you can be much more truthful in America about England than you can about America in America and vice versa but in spite of big business control of radio through advertisement-sponsored time on the air, writers and planners of programmes have a freer hand than in England.

There is of course much wider scope in America because an enormous amount of time daily must be filled: 7am to 2am generally with about twenty different programmes running at the same time. Studio executives are looking for writers who will accustom themselves to radio technique and regard radio writing as a literary and not a clerical occupation. In fact the heads of departments made a strong plea to the delegates to give the matter attention and arranged an afternoon session in each of two big studies where delegates could listen to playbacks of recorded dramas and discuss them with the directors.

I wish I could have heard Dorothy Parker speak on the Sophisticated Verse. She commenced by saying she knew nothing about it and ended by urging her audience to follow in the footsteps of Joe Hill, the International Workers of the World poet who, when he was being electrocuted for a murder he had not done, said, 'Don't mourn for me. Organise.' I believe the day of the individual is dead, she said. The future for writers lies in their ability to organise themselves and their colleagues in defence of the freedom which makes their craft possible.

At this session *The River,* a documentary film made by the New Deal Farming Administration and directed by Pare Lorentz, and rushes from a new uncompleted film showing the activities of the Ku Klux Klan against labour sympathisers, were shown. The latter is based on the findings of the La Follette Civil Liberties Investigation Committee.

The last session of the Congress was Writers in Exile, which was the least impressive. It amounted to a number of samey speeches and had little constructive to say on the way an author robbed of his country and his language could best work. The youngest refugee of all, Walter Schoenstedt, made the only concrete suggestion when he pointed out that writers could ally themselves with the colonies of foreign-born Americans which exist in every large city and find friendship and inspiration among them. Perhaps such action would prevent disasters like the suicide of Ernst Toller which occurred a couple of weeks back, shocking everyone who knew him.

My keen interest in the theatre made me want to know more about the Federal Theatre, part of the Works Progress Administration (WPA). I first went to see *Life and Death of an American* by George Sklar, which deals with the life of a boy, born with the century and killed in the Chicago Massacre when he was protesting with a couple of thousand other guys against a ten per cent wage cut. Sklar uses non-realistic technique and manages to present not only the narrow problem of a young man's life as it was done, say, in *Golden Boy*, where straight peep show techniques were used, but also to pose the wider problem of every struggling young American under a failing system. Especially does the chorus of four boys express young America wanting a decent life and finding only a raw deal.

Life and Death is one of the thousands of plays put on, in this and other cities all over America by the Federal Theatre, a section of the Works Progress Administration (WPA), which is President Roosevelt's scheme for employing and preserving the skill of America's workless. Roughly, WPA works like this. The Government sponsor schemes such as building low price housing projects, building roads, putting up schools and other public buildings, and the labour employed is recruited from those on the relief rolls. The projects themselves are actually carried out, or administered by, the State or City authority with grants from the Federal Government. For all WPA workers there is a maximum wage but skilled wages are paid for skilled work. In fact all wages paid are at the rates prevailing for the particular kind of work in this area. Thus a man who is a skilled labourer will have to work fewer hours to reach his maximum wage than an unskilled one. In this way one of the arguments against relief work, i.e. that it undercuts wages in commercial employment, is removed.

The Federal Theatre Project came into being because in 1935 there were thousands of unemployed actors, actresses, scene shifters, technicians and other theatre workers, partly due to the depression and partly due to the growing popularity and expansion of the cinema and the radio. Just as much as in the case of a skilled engineer who becomes unemployed and loses his skill as a consequence, so the actor and actress were losing theirs, and it was reckoned by the New Deal that skill is an important part of the national wealth.

Hallie Flanagan, a woman of talent and imaginative social understanding as well as of thorough experience in the theatre, became Director of the Theatre for the whole country, and Elmer Rice took over the New York City end. At first Rice was sceptical about the job and insisted that one dollar in ten which was allowed for other than labour costs would be inadequate for production costs. Other people were deterred for other reasons such as lack of theatrical talent among the unemployed, reasons which Rice thought nonsense but he was worried by the fact that the amount of plays the project could produce would employ only a fraction of those on the relief rolls. He was finally won over by Miss Flanagan when she suggested that the project could also produce living newspapers, dramatising current news with actors, music, movement and light. Rice went to work on the first issue of the newspaper, choosing Ethiopia as his subject. When rehearsals were already underway the State Department stepped up and said that no person was to represent any living foreign ruler on the stage, and in spite of the fact that the heads of the project explained that foreign rulers were in no way caricatured but merely presented in a purely factual way, the show had to be stopped. Rice resigned his position because he felt that this censorship was a ???? and would mean that no socially conscious plays would be acceptable to the State Department. Before he did so he protested against what he considered was interference with free expression.

The loss of Rice meant a certain setback but his protest did have some effect, and Federal Theatre has since produced much of real value theatrically as well as employing thousands of theatre people who would otherwise have starved on relief rolls.

Not only does the theatre produce plays in big towns and cities, they also maintain travelling units, a children's theatre, a theatre for the blind in Oklahoma, shows in prisons, schools, C.C.C. camps, asylums, and hospitals. The FTP has fought with the State Department and also with actors themselves. For instance, when *Triple-A Plowed Under* was in rehearsal they rebelled because they said the play, one about the wheat pit, the farmers, the price of milk and bread, gave no chance for anyone of the cast to make a big splash and name, but because they had been schooled in the star system and the three-act peepshow, middle-class drawing room play, about which the critics rave and the audience prattle small talk, they felt that real life had no place on the stage. After a heated discussion a bargain was struck. The actors agreed to give all they had for the present play, and those who were enthusiastic about this new form of theatre agreed that if it failed the Federal Theatre would give up all plans for future productions of the same character. The play went on not only in New York but in five other cities.

The Federal Theatre is not without enemies. Already the attack has been

JULY 1939

3C74

93

launched and the method of attack at this point is to yell about it being communist-red. You may ask why a theatre which strives to interest people in the things around them should be branded as red and wonder whether there can be any evidence for such allegations. The answer is that there is no such evidence. But reactionaries are always scared of anything new, anything which will make the people think for themselves, and the top and bottom of it is that the Federal Theatre has been too darned successful for the like of reactionary Senators like Mr Woodrum, who is leading the Republican attack against the New Deal. The attack on the Federal Theatre is just part of the strong attack which is being launched to discredit the New Deal so that the old lags can get themselves back into office when the 1940 elections come along.

It is proposed now to cut the theatre personnel by half all over the country and in New York City from 3,000 to 1,300 on 15 June and there is general protest not only from Actors Equity but from the general public and from supporters of New Deal itself.

Consider one fact and then ask yourself if the people of America want the Theatre Project and if they gain from it. Since its inception more than thirty million (30,000,000) [have been to a show], sixty-five per cent of whom (nineteen million, five hundred thousand) had never seen the living stage before. Or something more human – when I went to see *Life and Death of an American* it was two nights after seeing *The Little Foxes*. I had been impressed then by the character of the audience, alive, interested, and enthusiastic. But against the Federal Theatre audience they were like dummies – even if they were better dressed. Their enthusiasm paled in comparison with the undivided attention given to *Life and Death* because there were people seeing things which directly affected their lives, seeing people on the stage who were like themselves and with the same problems.

Another line of attack has been from those who say that FTP is unfair competition to the commercial theatre because it is subsidised and can therefore charge lower prices. What are the facts? In 1935, just one year before FTP was started, in New York City, the heart of theatre land, audiences had dwindled so that only seven of the 78 managers and directors in that city were operating at a profit. Today the theatre is in a healthier state largely due to FTP bringing life back into a near dead body. But still Mr Woodrum, Chairman of The Appropriations Committee of the House of Representatives, said 'Federal Theatre Project must go.' His sub committee set up to investigate, among other things, FTP did not have one witness from among those in a directorial capacity on the project and constantly gave credence to witnesses who gave totally inaccurate reports, not the least of which was a lie that ninety-nine percent of the FTP personnel had never worked in the theatre previously – a lie which can be disproved by the records.

Let Hallie Flanagan speak again. I quote from a letter she sent to Congressman Woodrum.

So much misinformation has been given to and by your investigators, I should like to give you the true perspective on Federal Theatre by asking you a few questions.

Have your investigators told you that ninety-five per cent of the persons on FTP come from relief rolls and if discharged would again face destitution?

Have they told you that the artistic caliber is so high that 2,650 of them have returned to private industry while the rest, according to competent critics, are working with increased skill?

Have they told you that the professional quality of FT's personnel is further attested not only by Broadway, Hollywood, and radio producers in hiring our people but by grants from various sources from the Rockefeller Foundation, the Guggenheim Foundation, Yale University, the University of North Carolina, Vassar College, the University of Syracuse, and many other educational institutions?

Have they told you that FTP has produced more than 1,200 plays?

Have they told you that the majority of these plays are former Broadway successes by American authors now given for the first time in communities unable to see them before; that other large classifications of our plays are the classics, children's plays, religious dramas, folk drama, marionette plays, musical comedies and plays by hitherto unknown American authors?

Have they told you that sixty-five per cent of these plays are given free to under-privileged groups in schools, hospitals, prisons, social settlement centres, homes for the aged, and other public institutions, the inmates of which are not able to afford entertainment?

Have they told you that the artistic achievement of these projects, while not satisfactory completely to our directors and actors who share with me the desire for continued improvement, have nevertheless won acclaim from leading dramatic critics?

Have they enquired of professional dramatic critics as to the artistic quality of the project? Isn't it possible that these gentlemen, by reason of their training and standards of comparison and by virtue of the fact they have reviewed plays we have done, are in a better position than anyone else to judge whether Federal Theatre is of value to the American Theatre scene?

Has your committee, may I ask, made a study of the human values of the FTP, of some of the people saved from destitution and despair, restored to health and self-respect and able to provide for themselves and their families and live again as paying members of a community?

It is my understanding that it was the business of your committee to find the truth about FTP. Yet on 7 June you are quoted by the *New York Times* as saying 'They (the communists) are running the projects.' Does not this put you in the position of giving the press your conclusions before examining all pertinent evidence?

To Congressman Woodrum, the FTP is one small branch of a great work program designed to give useful employment to professionally qualified people. It is not now and never has been run by any political party. It is administered by properly appointed and professionally qualified representatives of the government of the United States. These representatives are still waiting to place in your hands the record of the Federal Theatre – on which it stands.

Sincerely yours,
Hallie Flanagan.

So, the American Theatre is fighting for its life, because it's a cinch that if they scrap Federal Theatre they will just be putting another dagger in the back of the commercial theatre. Of course it is not only the theatre they are cracking against. Woodrum and his Republican friends would like to wipe out the whole of the WPA but they daren't. Not yet anyway. It would mean too many people on the breadline too soon after they had known something better.

Our quest for jazz played as negroes only can play it led us first to Café Society in New York, newly opened by John Henry Hammond, one of America's foremost jazz critics and talent scout for a number of record companies. The band there was led by Frankie Newton, who used to play for Mezz Mezzrow and many other well-known bands. Café Society is rather an up-town place but just cheap enough for us to pay for drinks if we are careful.

Efforts to get into joints in the deep south were fairly unsuccessful. Proprietors were sympathetic but told us that as soon as a white woman stepped inside his place the police would come in and smash the place up, screaming rape. We did get into one or two and it was a sheer joy to hear real Negro jazz with no gloss of publicity-seeking on it. Not so good but better than we heard in England was the Savoy ballroom in Harlem where we went with a Negro friend. A huge place with a 'big' band, very commercial and packed full of dancers. I liked the way people danced. Not keeping together as we did at home but often leaving their partners to improvise their own steps.

In my search for material about the trial of Sacco and Vanzetti,* two Italians caught in a police trap and charged with murder, I met Tom O'Connor, a man who made the study of the case his life's work. I had two three hour meetings with him, and he paid me the complement of saying that I knew more about the case than anyone he had met excluding those involved in the case at the time. I met Herbert Ehrmann, a lawyer who defended Sacco and Vanzetti in the later stages of the trial.

Because I am interested in anything to do with Sacco and Vanzetti I went to see Winterset, a film based on a book by Maxwell Anderson, made in 1936 with Burgess Meredith in the main part. The film is a poetic drama which is quite impressive and much praised by the critics although in later years they changed their minds and panned it.

'The way people dress strikes me as much more sensible than in England.' That is what I wrote sixty odd years ago. I thought them less formal in their dress especially the men. I found them wearing all sorts of odd and fancy clothing.

Women were better dressed than at home and there is no doubt that a very conscious attempt is made by the designers of women's clothes to make women more sexually attractive. With the result that even plain women appear quite glamorous, especially in artificial light. American men and, I suppose, some women, claimed that America was a woman's country. In the sense that women did all the shopping, not just the tea and sugar but the furniture, pianos, life insurance, houses and motor cars. They also controlled the social engagements of their husbands. Men spent a lot of cash on their women and gave them the sort of respect the rich give to their servants, which means complete subservience. Women were really complete dirt and got none of the attention an intelligent woman expects. No one listens to them. I found a good deal of this attitude among the people I met who for the most part were the progressive middle-class. You had to fight your way in and convince them you have something to say before you get a hearing.

Women were definitely barred from some cafés and saloons. It is a little difficult to say which because there is no 'Gentlemen Only' sign; it is much more a matter of knowing from practice. Some of the ones which might be expected to exclude women did not and exhibited a notice saying 'Ladies Invited'. There were of course some quite innocuous bars which do not admit women and into one of these James and I popped one day. We sat up at the counter and the bar man said 'sorry no women' and James thought he meant not at the counter so we moved over to a wall seat. 'Didn't you hear me say no dames bud?' said the bar man, and we had to back out.

* Nicola Sacco and Bartolomeo Vanzetti were Italian immigrants and anarchists. Sacco, a shoe worker, and Vanzetti, a fish peddler, were accused of the murder... of a paymaster and his guard on 15 April 1920, during a payroll robbery at a shoe factory in Braintree, Mass. Contradictory evidence in the 1921 trial and the pair's subsequent execution on 22 August 1927, by the electric chair, elevated them to martyr status in the Italian anarchist movement.

The Communist Party of USA supported President Roosevelt and his New Deal policies very energetically. The Party knows that he may fail to take his support for the people to the last fence but at the moment he was playing a progressive role against the reactionaries both Republicans and Democrats in Roosevelt's own party who were the instigators of such things as the Woodrum Bill which, when it goes through Congress, will make the following wrecking cuts to the WPA plans.

Cut WPA Rolls by one third and leave most families affected destitute as most states do not pay out relief to able bodied.

This attack on WPA is the first big punch at the New Deal and it looks as though it will strike home. Roosevelt of course could refuse to sign the Bill even when both houses have passed it but if he did that it would mean that there would be no money at all for WPA until another Bill was passed through and in the meantime people would starve.

From August 1935 with a little over a quarter of a million persons on the rolls, to May 1939 when the numbers were 2,527,943, the Nation has spent over seven thousand million dollars (7,110,786,000) on WPA, a good deal of which has been borrowed. The Republicans have accused Roosevelt of getting into debt and his answer has sometimes been 'When a company borrows money it is called expansion, when a country borrows it is called getting into debt.'

And look what America has to show from this borrowing. The jokes about WPA workers leaning on shovels and doing nothing but boondoggle (i.e. filling up holes they have dug themselves for no particular purpose) are awarded by these achievements.

Education: More than 34,000 teachers on WPA are giving two million adults a better education. 1,494 nursery schools take care of 50,000 pre-school children. Under WPA one million Americans have learned to write. American school children have eaten 23,000,000 lunches free, cooked by WPA women.

Recreation: WPA has increased recreation facilities by 15,000 parks and playgrounds, 696 swimming pools, 357 golf courses, 6,433 tennis courts, 9,328 recreational buildings.

Theatre and Music Federal Theatre units play to an audience of twelve million annually, there are 13,596 performers; 132,243,800 people heard 202,488 concerts by the music project; 9,627 musicians were involved. They played 6,277 compositions, 2,034 of which were by American composers.

Libraries: WPA librarians have catalogued 27 million books; eight thousand new branch libraries are staffed by WPA workers; 29 million books have been renovated; 73 new libraries have been built, 654 improved or enlarged; 1,100 travelling libraries carry the luxury of books to remote areas.

Blind: Over two million pages of braille have been transcribed by WPA workers. WPA is responsible for the only braille encyclopaedia available in English.

Art: American art has gained a wealth of additional work from WPA art projects. Public galleries, community centres and public buildings have had 3,562 pieces of sculpture by WPA workers; 48,000 easel paints, 1,345 murals and mosaics are in tax supported institutions. 84,340 prints, etchings, lithographs, woodblocks etc are available for distribution to schools, hospitals and other public buildings. WPA workers staff 68 community art centres.

Architectural Records: Jobless architects and draftsmen on the American Building survey have measured and recorded details of 2,300 famous buildings. They have made 16,000 drawings and17,000 photographs which are available at a nominal charge at the Library of Congress.

Airports: The progress of aviation has been materially aided by WPA. Its workers have constructed 202 hangars, 400 miles of runways and 10,000 air markers.

Rural Construction: Rural roads totaling 268,000 miles have been constructed. Work on bridges aggregates 352 miles, or the distance from New York to Youngstown Ohio. This includes 20,000 new bridges and improvement of 23,000 already standing.

Public Buildings: A total of 65,543 public buildings including schools, hospitals, have been constructed. 17,562 have been reconstructed. 46,318 have been repaired and renovated. 1,663 have been added to.

I was most impressed by Eleanor Roosevelt, not as the President's wife but because of the sound sense she spoke and the way she seemed to grasp the problems of the Congress.

Her speech was friendly and contained not only a good deal of political sense but many concrete hints to these delegates on how to better run their conference, a point which showed that she really has been taking an interest in the various sessions of the Congress which she has attended. 'I do not pretend to know all the answers to the problems which beset our country,' she said, 'but we find that when they are brought into the light and discussed a solution is found. I am not one of those who are afraid to let youth come together and discuss although I am aware that there are people in our country who are so afraid.'

'I believe,' she said, 'that one day because there are people in organisations like yours wanting to get something done, we shall have a state where we do not have to use force as we do today. I want to see a great campaign for knowledge in this country. There are things happening all over the Union which if people knew about then, they would protest vigorously. The unemployed for instance. We have done something for our unemployed but not enough. There are people who say we have done too much, that if there are those who cannot get a job in their own trade they should take some other, and that the WPA schemes for putting people to work at their own trade are against the interests of the people. But what if these people have lost their jobs through no fault of their own and can do no other work. What then? Are they to starve? And are we to kill our national skill by forcing people to work at jobs for which they are not fitted?'

As we move further south the negro to white ratio becomes greater but this does not mean that things are better for the negro. On the contrary, they are worse. Although the Civil War rid the United States of slavery it did not produce any legislation which said negroes must be paid a living wage, nor did it assure that negroes should have at least as good treatment as white men and women. Consequently the negroes are the most exploited section of the community. On top of the general exploitation of every man and woman under capitalism, the negroes suffer an additional amount of repressiveness because of their colour.

The country we are passing through is edging on the tobacco growing area and we see a lot of growing, mostly small plots owned by tenant farmers or farms owned by big guys and worked by sharecroppers. No crop no share, no share no money to buy food. The other crops around here are corn and a little cotton, but actually we are not far enough south for the real big cropping area.

Our trip to the South was a revelation. We hoped to get as far as Birmingham, Alabama which we did, lingering on the way around the various dams. Norris Dam, Chickamauga, and now Chattanooga in the state of Tennessee. It used to be a dry state but the people wanted liquor and so they made a cross on the paper and the town was no longer dry. We understood not dry meant wet but it was not quite like that. All along the street there are liquor shops but no bars. Positively none. You can buy a bottle of corn whisky for one dollar (there were four dollars to the pound in those days) and Scotch will cost you about twice that much but it's all there in these huge liquor shops displaying big neon signs and open till 11 pm.

We thought the idea was to take your bottle into a restaurant, order soda and drink your whisky. We tried it and managed it in one place but at the next we nearly got arrested and had to smuggle the stuff out in a handbag. We had ordered four cokes and four sodas but what we got was four cokes and the manager of the place setting his watch dogs on us. So out we came. You see what the law says is that you can buy the liquor but you cannot drink it until you get home. Got to get it right home before you break the seal. Because what the vote did was to change Chattanooga into a package town. As much drink as you like but not in public. But here is the funny thing. Right on the best corner of the best street in town is a hotel called the Oregon. Five hundred bedrooms, every one with a bath, and the rates start at three dollars a day for a room only.

Now in this town you can get a drink of whisky in a glass any time of the day or night and no policeman appears. At one place only. Three guesses for the name of it.

On our way here from Washington we have come through some very fine country. Huge mountain ranges one moment and downs the next. And the sunsets are glorious, pale colours, and seen from the top of a mountain they are unforgettable. We stopped off at Norris Dam the other night and we were all impressed by its beauty and size and by the way it had been developed from just a dam to a real place of social construction.

In 1936 Norris Dam was finished in front of schedule having been started in the autumn of 1933. Its power installation is 132,000 horsepower and the roadway along the top is over a mile long. The reservoir formed behind the dam covers 34,000 acres and you can swim and boat in it. Before the dam could be built 275,000 cubic yards of rock and 170,000 cubic yards of earth had to be excavated. These are figures, at first sight meaningless, but think of them in terms of your own garden and the amount of earth you would have to remove to make a pond six feet deep wide and long (216 cubic feet of earth) and then look at those figures again.

Around the dam a model town has been built, with frame houses, a drug store, some shops, a school, and some apartment houses. Here live the people who are working on the upkeep of the dam and in the tourist camp which is built on one of the nearby slopes and overlooks the dam. Also in the town live those who are working on the soil conservation scheme and water control which helps the farmers in this valley to nourish their impoverished soil.

Flood control is a big problem in these parts. Not only the floods you see i.e. the swollen river and the swamped ground but the small floods, the rain coming down over a dry soil, devoid of trees and other growths, carrying the top soil with it and rendering the land useless for growing purposes not only while the rain lasts but for years afterwards. These are floods you do not see.

In Tennessee, nearly 6,000 tons of water fall on every acre every year. Because the land around here has been misused, because any farmer with wood on his land has been forced by economic reasons to cut it down and sell it, and because land owners and speculators have not given a care to what happens to the land, they have chopped off the top of the trees which act as a deterrent to floods of this kind and neglected to plant plants which help to keep the top on the soil and hold the water in the hills. If you can't see these floods you can surely see the results in the poor land, the gullied slopes, the disintegrating homesteads, and the poverty stricken people in a land which is potentially rich.

We talked last night to the organiser of the Farmers Union in this town and surrounding district. He was once a preacher but he got kicked out because of his activities on behalf of the farmers. Preaching here is a funny business. It works like this. A guy sets up as a preacher and gets people to subscribe to his salary, both by collections and rich men's subscriptions. As long as he talks the kind of stuff the rich boys like he gets his money but when he begins to tell that they are a lousy lot of profiteers, the money dries up and that's what happened to our guy, Rock.

The Communist Party in Birmingham, which is a fairly large industrial town, is ninety per cent black, fifty per cent of whom are illiterate. They are mostly men and women who work in the cotton mills in the town, and there are very few middle-class people even among the whites.

One of the biggest fights is for black votes, and the abolition of the poll tax. There is no law which says blacks may not vote but they are kept away from the polls pretty successfully in the following manner. Everyone over twenty-one has to register and receive a certificate before he can be put on the voting list. Registration entails visiting the town hall and if a black tries to get in he either gets a knock on the back of his neck as he goes up the steps by some anti-black swine or if he gets inside he is intimidated so that he leaves pretty quickly. If he gets as far as applying for a certificate he is told it will be sent through the post. He goes home more or less satisfied and never hears another word.

Another measure working not only against blacks who are among the poorest members of the community but also against poor whites is the poll tax. Each year every adult has to pay three dollars poll tax without a receipt for which he cannot vote. Now if you do not pay your poll tax in 1940, say, you have to pay two years in 1941 if you want to vote which means that those people who have let their poll tax slide for any length of time can never afford to pay off the back taxes and are consequently deprived of a vote.

Just recently a victory in the votes for blacks campaign was won. A few thousand blacks filled in blanks for registration and as usual they heard nothing more about their applications. A young black lawyer filed a petition against the state on their behalf and although the Judge refused to hear the case within a month every black who had made an application got his certificate. Now the blacks feel more confidence and roll up to the town hall and demand that they get certificates and although there is a good deal of beating up round side streets by such organisations as the Ku Klux Klan, the American Legion, and the Vigilante groups, no black has so far been assaulted near the town hall whilst on his way to sign.

The next question will arise at the next election. Will blacks manage to get to the polling booths without being beaten up and how many of them will be intimidated by the activities of the groups I have mentioned above?

Looking back I think the America of the late-thirties was very like Britain of the seventies. The Americans were first with casual dress; they were first with casual behaviour as well as first with a whole lot of other nastier things like drugs and massive petty crime. One area in which the Americans were way behind Britain was their attitude to women. America has often been called a women's country but that means women are treated like dolls and precious china. 'I vote the same way as my husband does.' 'My husband says Roosevelt is a rotten president and I agree with him.' These sorts of remarks I heard every day. At least that was the way it was in New York and in Chicago. In California women were less the 'worst half' of their husbands in the circles I moved in. Maybe they were not typical as most of the people I knew in Los Angeles were refugees from Germany.

Bank of England,

London, E.C.2.

6th August, 1941.

Dear Arnold,

Nancie Elizabeth Whittaker

    I am obliged to you for your letter of the 30th July (P.F.52673/W.3.Air) with further reference to the case of Miss N.E.Whittaker.

    I note that after further considera- tion you adhere to the recommendation affecting Miss N.E.Whittaker as set out in the letter dated the 8th July 1941 (P.F.52673/D.S.C.3) addressed by your Mr.H.W.H.Sams to Pearce.

    In the circumstances, the Bank are dispensing with the services of Miss N.E.Whittaker.

    I am,

      Yours sincerely,

[signature]

104
Squadron Leader Henry Arnold.

At my request, Mr. Sams made an enquiry from the Ministry of Information. They said that Nancy WHITTAKER left in June, 1944 and that shortly before that date she had become Mrs. BERGER. She is now believed to be living with Roland BERGER @ SHEPHERD, at 7, St.Katherine's Precincts, Regents' Park, N.W.1.

13th July, 1944.
F.2.a   David K. Clarke.

VIII
Back to Britain and War

Telephone No.
EUSton 4321.

Telegrams :—
" MINIFORM, LONDON."

  *Any further communication
should be addressed to :—*
  The Director General
*and the following reference should
be quoted :—*

MINISTRY OF INFORMATION,

MALET STREET,

LONDON, W.C.1.

8th October, 1941.

Dear Sams,

We are rather disturbed about your letter
(PF.52673/C3) of the 3rd October about Miss
Nancy Whitaker. She is employed, generally
speaking, on non-confidential work but we
cannot guarantee that she will not have access
in her present post to some confidential
material. Satisfactory references were given
by Mr. A.E. Douglas-Smith of the Board of
Extramural Studies, University of Cambridge,
and by Mr. Arnold Watson of 61, Alexandria
Road, Southport, an officer of the Ministry of
Labour.

In the circumstances I should be very
grateful if you could give me more detailed
information about the nature of your objections
to her employment.

Yours sincerely,

C.S.

H. W. H. Sams, Esq.,
Box 500,
    G. P. O.,
       Oxford.

MY STAY IN AMERICA was cut short because of the imminence of war. I sailed on the *SS Washington*, an American owned ship, and two days at sea brought the news of the declaration of war by Britain on Germany. The ship was covered with American flags and seemed to be going very slowly.

One day, about three days after we sailed, the ship started turning back and at 6pm we learnt from the captain that we were steaming to the rescue of the survivors of a British ship which had been torpedoed by a German submarine. At 10pm we got to the spot and saw flares going up. Having shown no enthusiasm for the war, by this time the passengers were all highly excited and were talking about getting their hands round the neck of a German. We picked up about thirty men and a canary which belonged to the third mate. There was more sympathy for the bird than for the sailors. When the sailors had been given a bath and a meal they were turned loose on the third class passengers who stood them numerous drinks. Soon, the anti-Nazi feeling engendered by the rescue had almost completely changed to respect for the German Commander of the submarine who had allowed the sailors to leave the ship before it was sunk and had sent up the flares that had guided us to pick them up. When they were given a drink, they said 'Drink to the Commander. A real gentleman.' The British ship which was sunk was the *SS Olivegrove*, registered in Glasgow and carrying a cargo of 6,000 tons of sugar from Cuba. The submarine which we saw in the moonlight as it disappeared over the horizon was painted a dull grey and showed no markings. The sailors said that the Commander, a man of around twenty-eight, could speak fairly good English and had asked them why Chamberlain had turned on them since he was normally very generous towards Germany.

Six of the crew of the *Olivegrove* were Indians and they were completely ignored by the other sailors and passengers. The sailors complained that they were cowards and that they had lain in the bottom of the lifeboat for the whole of the eight hours that they were adrift. One sailor explained to me that, in their normal work, the Indians rarely saw the sea as they were confined to the galley, getting no training or instruction in seamanship at all. It was a survival instinct for them to get to the bottom of the lifeboat.

When the ship arrived at Southampton there was a thick fog and we were marooned for some hours which added to the mystery of what blackout and war was all about. Eating in Lyons Corner House in the Strand on my first night home I was surprised to see people cheering anyone in uniform and clapping and singing when a sailor or soldier came into the restaurant. It did not feel right to me. I knew very little about war. I had been born in 1914, so the First World War was a bit remote but I do remember the Zeppelins over Manchester and a bit more clearly talk about building of the British R33 and R34, copies that had been made possible by the capture of a German L33. The British copies were not complete until 1919, after the war was over. I was of course very aware of the Spanish war but since the British were only indirectly involved because of the volunteers in the International Brigades and through the diplomatic stance which had made it possible for the German and Italians to send arms to Franco but prevented the Spanish elected government getting any arms, I had no experience of a fighting war affecting the daily lives of people.

The only sort of war I knew anything about was the class war, the struggle between the people and the factory owners and other capitalists; between the people and a government which was pauperising the workers through cuts in all kinds of benefits and failing to take action against the rise in prices of essential foods. I had marched as a soldier in this way, with the unemployed when they entered London on their long trek from the industrial cities of the north, I had worked long hours, collecting money in order to give the marchers some food and drink, mainly bangers, bread and tea, and I had helped to collect clothes and household provisions as well as toys for the children.

Class war was something I could understand and relate to. I felt part of it even though the enemy could be identified only in general terms and after careful analysis. Allies in the class war could be recognised but even they might change with a changing situation. The war I came into when I returned from the United States was one which could be called a fighting war. War with an identifiable enemy, a war for which I should have been able to feel enthusiastic because it was against Hitler and, so we thought at the time, against fascism. But I could not feel any enthusiasm for it and I wondered if it was because at heart I was still a pacifist, a position I thought I had rejected when my brother, with my agreement and approval, had joined the International Brigades. I was uncertain about the nature of the war. I felt quite strongly that it was unlikely that Neville Chamberlain, the prime minister who had avowed his friendship with Hitler and demonstrated this friendship with his actions, would really fight fascism with any real determination.

So, when I saw people in large cafés such as Lyons Corner House in the Strand waving Union Jacks and singing patriotic songs I felt uneasy and could not join in. In spite of its declared intentions – to fight Hitler – I did not feel it was *my* war, even though the political body to which I belonged, the Communist Party, supported the war as a war against fascism. It was calling on the workers and the people of the country to support it, a political line to which I had subscribed.

Their support for the war was explained in a statement issued by the Central Committee of the Party which designated the war as the 'most cruel and unnecessary in history', and urged the people to wage struggle on two fronts, firstly one to secure military victory over fascism and secondly, and in order to achieve this, one to secure the political victory over Chamberlain. 'The Communist Party stresses that fascism should be defeated. Get rid of Chamberlain and the view of Munich and the stronger your fight against Hitler,' wrote Harry Pollitt, the General Secretary of the Party, in a penny pamphlet, published in 50,000 copies. It went more deeply into the question of why communists should support a war between two capitalist countries, under the leadership of Chamberlain, who had refused to help Austria, in spite of Hitler's threats to invade. At the time he had stated that, 'We must not delude small, weak nations into thinking they will be protected by the League [of Nations] against aggression.' A month later Hitler's troops had marched into Austria.

Hitler then set his sights on Czechoslovakia, a country more protected than Austria through a full military assistance pact with France and a limited one with the Soviet Union. The view of the Communist Party was that Britain should join this mutual assistance pact but Chamberlain and his government refused to even discuss such a scheme. Certain sections of the British press were accusing Chamberlain of encouraging Hitler to invade Czechoslovakia. After much negotiation and concessions concerning the Sudeten Germans in Czechoslovakia, the threat was apparently delayed while Chamberlain went to Hitler's retreat in Berchtesgaden, a journey which Willie Gallacher, the Communist MP for West Fife, said was a journey to betray peace not save it.

A week later in September, Chamberlain went again to see Hitler at Godesberg and was met with demands of a more extreme nature than those discussed at Berchtesgaden including the evacuation by the Czechs from all of the military and industrial installations in Sudeten which were to be left intact. The Czechs rejected the plan and started mobilisation. Later in September when Chamberlain returned from Munich he was met by cheering crowds. The paper he held up in the air represented, he said, 'Peace in our time'. A few months later his treachery was exposed. The Germans entered Prague and Hitler was able to announce that Czechoslovakia had ceased to exist.

Our one member of Parliament, Willie Gallacher, made the only speech against the betrayal.

'No one desires peace more than I and my Party,' he said, 'but it must be peace based on freedom and democracy and not upon the cutting up and destruction of a small State. I want to say that the policy of the National Government has led to this crisis, yes! and if there is peace at the moment it is the determined attitude of the people that has saved it. Whatever the outcome, the National Government will have to answer for its policy, I would not be a party to what is going on here. There are as many fascists opposite as there are in the Germany, and I protest against the dismemberment of Czechoslovakia.'

I well remember the day when Hitler announced that Czechoslovakia was no more. I was listening to the radio with a friend. 'The beginning of the end,' he said, 'from now on we are in a different ball game.' How right he was.

At the time when the country was full of rumours and stories, good and bad, one sticks in my mind. In the talks between Chamberlain and the Czech Ambassador in London, Chamberlain told him that Britain would take action to protect his country *if* this happened or *if* that happened. Sickened by his attitude the Ambassador said, 'You mean if my aunt had balls she'd be my uncle.'

During this crisis the government made many moves towards putting Britain on a war footing. The Naval fleet was mobilised, territorials were called up, gas masks were distributed and school children evacuated. Speaking from the platform at the 15th Congress of the Communist Party on 16–18 September 1938, Rajani Palme Dutt, member of the Central Committee, said, 'No one who has followed events in the past few weeks can fail to see that the Government has been deliberately encouraging a certain warmonger.'

For the next twelve months life in the Communist parties of the world was pretty hectic. One crisis followed another, and I seemed to be on the streets more often than I was getting a hot dinner even when I was in the USA. Hitler had his sights on Poland. The Communist Party continued to demand that the British sign a mutual assistance pact with France and the Soviet Union. The Soviet Union itself proposed consultation between some foreign nations: the Soviet Union, Britain, France, Romania, Poland and Turkey, but Chamberlain's government refused. Later he proposed a triple defensive alliance of France, Britain and the USSR, declining to propose guarantees to Romania and Poland. Eventually a Foreign Office official was sent to Moscow to discuss the pact. In contrast to Chamberlain's response to Hitler's demands and his personal journeys to Germany, this time his government sent an 'old boy' who played in 'the Munich team', and who delayed his visit time and time again before finally rushing off to Moscow by train. Negotiations dragged on, and hope that there could be peace got thinner and thinner. Then on 23 August 1939 the Soviets took a step which astounded everyone and they signed a non-aggression pact with Hitler's Germany.

I was in California living in a 'colony' of refugees from Europe when this news broke, amongst whom were writers, film makers and many others who had first fled to Spain, and then to the USA when the Spanish war broke out. I well remember the consternation among them when news of the Nazi–Soviet pact came through. They could not think rationally about it and felt personally betrayed, even though most of them had never lifted a finger to help or protect the USSR. Only a few were prepared to discuss the implications of the pact, and one or two could see that it was a tactical move by the Soviet Union in order to gain time to strengthen itself to meet the Nazi onslaught which they were sure would come. The film director Fritz Lang had a more or less sensible view. They were all, of course, fearful of internment and the pact seemed to bring that moment nearer, and, in response, they increased their hunts for wives who would protect them. I never heard whether they found wives or were interned.

The Communist Party campaigned from morning till night on the issue of getting France, the Soviet Union, and Poland together for a real peace initiative but the reaction to the Nazi–Soviet pact was so sharp that the USSR was no longer regarded, by the majority of the British population, as a country interested in peace for the Western world.

On 1 September 1939, Hitler invaded Poland. On 3 September Chamberlain declared war against Germany. Despite the change in its position, the Communist Party had been behind the war effort and had encouraged its young members to join up many months before the due date for their call-up. It was especially keen to see that party members

with some military experience or training joined the forces to fight the
war it described as a joint war against fascism. My brother Peter, who
had experience in Spain as well as training in an Officer Training School
connected with his school, joined up, leaving his studies at the LSE for
the second time.

But the support for the war by the Communist Party did not last long.
Many members were uneasy about supporting a war between two capitalist countries, although the vast majority of the Party were to support the
war in various practical ways as well as giving general support. The signs
were that not every Communist Party agreed with the line of the British
Party: the CPUSA declared the war an important one; the Soviet Union
in various broadcasts referred to the war as imperialist and predatory on
both sides. In the British branches there was confusion and tremendous
discussion. I remember sitting up late night after night discussing the
situation and coming to no conclusion.

But the progress of the war – rapid advance by the German army
into Poland and the fact that the Soviet army had crossed the Polish
border and occupied the eastern half of Poland – meant that the central
committee had to reconsider its position. Palme Dutt was in favour of
changing the 'line', while Pollitt and Johnny Campbell, then editor of the
Daily Worker, were in favour of continuing the support for the war.
Dave Springhall, who had been the representative on the Communist
International in Moscow arrived with the message that the Communist

International believed the war to be an imperialist one and that the working-class movement in the world should give it no support and even oppose it.

After endless discussions, gradually the other members of the Central Committee of the Communist Party came to accept the Comintern's interpretation of the war. Pollitt and Campbell, however, remained unconvinced.

Pollitt, a boilermaker by trade, gave up his position as General Secretary and headed to his native Lancashire to look for a job. The shipbuilding yards where he could be expected to find a job in his trade were already controlled by the Admiralty. A retired admiral in charge of one where Harry applied said that he had no intention of employing a communist at the shipyard and told him to get off the premises. Instead Harry sought out the chief shop steward of the yard and explained to him what had happened. Without a word the shop steward strode off to confront the Admiral and in no uncertain terms made it clear that he'd be without any boilermakers unless Politt was employed. Harry got work the same day.

In November 1939, the Comintern, headed by George Dimitrov, the anti-fascist hero of the Leipzig Trial, issued a manifesto outlining its opposition to the war. Herbert Morrison, a leading anti-communist crusader, as well as other leaders of the Labour Party, declared that the Communist Party's revision of policy would spell doom for its membership, projecting that large numbers would leave the Party. In fact the Party gained a great many new members at this time. It led to the Party declaring that the people of Britain would defeat the imperialists and capitalists and that this would encourage the German workers to rise up against Hitler. While neither of these things happened, either at this stage or later in the war, what did happen was that a considerable body opposing the war became vocal. The *Daily Worker* reported anti-war resolutions passed by trade union branches, local Labour Party branches, co-operative organisations, and women's groups. Meetings called by the Communist Party drew record attendances, and when the magazine *Labour Monthly,* edited by a leading Communist, called a conference to discuss the war situation around 900 delegates attended representing some thousands of people throughout the labour movement.

Discussion continued in the Communist Party itself and often became quite bitter, though the public saw only a united front, which some found confusing. The reason for the unity within the Party was due to the way in which the Party operated regarding decisions. Bodies within the Party, groups, branches, district committees and of course the executive committee, discussed every issue in detail but once a decision was made it became obligatory for every member to operate in accordance with the decision. This was necessary, in the opinion of the Party, in order to maintain a united front against the enemy. Remembering that the Party considered itself at all times engaged in a class war against the ruling class, this was an acceptable method of procedure, and while it imposed hard discipline on those who had disagreements it made for greater operational efficiency.

Nevertheless, the Party was frequently criticised for being an undemocratic body and its members named toadies of Moscow. The Party was also accused of taking money from the Soviet Union and when I was a branch official searching round for enough cash to pay the gas bill in the Party rooms I often wished it were true. What was true was that from the start of the *Daily Worker*, the Soviet Union had bought thousands of copies every day which it resold to the European countries. It was in effect a subsidy, and it lasted in one form or another until the late eighties. When the Soviet Union collapsed and various public papers were released, it was revealed in 1992 that the Soviet Union had made, over the years, gifts of money to the Communist Party.

The press made a meal out of this 'revelation' though personally was not shocked nor even surprised. That the first socialist country in the world should give money to Communist Parties in capitalist countries such as Britain, which was likely to be practically the last country to go socialist, seemed to me to be expected.

While there was support within the labour movement for the Party's opposition to the war there was also an increase in the abuse that the Party and its individual members suffered. When in November 1939 the Soviet Union invaded Finland, the opposition and the abuse increased. It was almost impossible to discuss the matter with people, and useless to explain that the invasion was to protect Leningrad, which was only twenty miles from the Finnish border and therefore at risk should the war spread.

Not only was the Party abused but steps were taken by the authorities to make life difficult for the members of the Party and indeed for all left wing groups and individuals. The Party itself realised the dangers ahead and took steps to safeguard its resources and members in so far as it could. Some members were withdrawn from Party branches and organised in small groups. Some of the groups were given tasks to do but they were not very onerous and they were instructed to study the behaviour of other parties which had been forced to operate under semi-illegal conditions. I happened to be one of the 'withdrawn' people. I could be spared from the general struggle as I was neither a key industrial worker nor an experienced organiser. In fact, I was a rather frightened ambulance driver, stationed in Islington, watching night after night for bombs to fall. On the day shift I learned first aid and how to load an injured body on to an ambulance stretcher. I hoped very much that I should never have to do the real thing as I got very upset at the sight of blood. I prayed there would never be a bomb when I was on duty and carried on with my work as a non-card holding communist, buying stocks of paper, reading books on the underground work of European parties, and studying Clausewitz's writing *On War*. It all seemed very important at the time as much of my thinking was directed towards the possibility of uncovering a fifth column which I reckoned was being organised somewhere. Chamberlain had, to a large extent, let the ruling class down by going to war against Germany, as for many of them Hitler and the Nazis were really their friends, and it seemed more than likely that someone, somewhere, was preparing a group of pro-Nazi people for a fascist take-over of Britain at the appropriate time. That no such discovery was made by our group was not for the lack of hard searching. We did find out about groups of pro-fascists but they were composed mainly of nit-witted upper-class people who knew nothing of war or politics.

All this work I was doing seemed important at the time and I still believe it was because it taught anti-fascists to look beyond the open, overt fascist movements to the more subtle machinations of the ruling class.

I escaped the bombs by getting a job in the Bank of England starting in the department which sorted photo-data of intercepted mail which indicated that the sender or receiver had interests overseas which they had not declared under the regulation which forbade such holdings. I was called a 'clerk' as were the vast majority of women who worked there. Later I got a position in a small unit set up to examine Britain's balance of payment with various countries. At this time the information was 'classified'.

I could not help enjoying working at the Bank though I could see the essential horror of it. The conditions were so good: well ventilated offices, good desks and seating, free lunches, and a super nursing service. And later, when the bombs began to fall on the city, protection in what was probably the most solid building in the City of London. To reduce the travel on the part of staff the Bank organised shift work. We worked from 9 am to 8 pm on day one, had dinner in the bank and slept in the vaults in truckle beds with reading lights. On day two the routine was the same. On day three we finished at 7 pm, had dinner and went home until day six when the cycle started again. So, in three days, one did thirty-two hours work, had two sleeps, two lunches and two dinners. The week was

Monday to Saturday. It suited the Bank who got a lot of work out of the employees. It suited the employees by easing travelling and cooking and gave them four days off out of every six.

The Bank had rather peculiar ideas about male–female relationships perhaps because the Bank corridors and offices were a sort of marriage market. Females employed by the Bank had to be sponsored by a director although not necessarily personally known – a friend of a friend of a friend would suffice. This meant they were suitable wives for the men working there and vice versa. Females were not allowed into offices where only one man was working. When a colleague and myself were doing a piece of research which meant interviewing many men it was not enough that there were two of us though only one of him. We had a senior woman clerk allocated to us to make up the party. I don't think she brought her knitting with her but she might just as well have done so since she understood nothing of the matter under discussion.

Whilst the Bank had an 'internal' union for the permanent staff, nothing had been done to give the temporary clerks any means of expressing their grievances. As the number of temporary clerks, almost all women, was increasing all the time, the bank looked favourably on anyone who had suggestions as to how they could be given the same rights as permanent clerks without joining the permanent company union.

A colleague of mine working in the balance of payments unit suggested to the authorities that the temporary clerks should have a 'committee' to represent them and that she and I would work out a constitution and a method of recruitment. Mr Holland Martin agreed with this proposal and put a car at our disposal so we could visit the Bank's evacuated outposts, and himself arranged at least two 'mass' meetings at headquarters.

Ironically, the first case this committee had to cope with was the 'unfair sacking' of its elected chair – myself. One day about six weeks after the committee was elected and the organisation was taking up various staff complaints such as unfair treatment of people who arrived late, I was called to the office of the high chief of the Bank's personnel department at 4.55pm, and kept waiting until 5.15pm, fifteen minutes after everyone had left the building, and preventing me from making contact with any of my colleagues.

I was instructed to collect any belongings I had and leave the Bank at once. The reason? That I was living with a close friend of Harry Pollitt, and that I had been a Communist Party member for some years and a security risk for the bank. The Temporary Women Clerks Committee did take up the case at once but the Bank had little difficulty persuading the members that I was a red menace.

I do not think the Bank sacked me because I tried to organise temporary clerks in an organisation. I think they had me followed and discovered that the friends I had were 'unsuitable' for a bank employee and in
some cases highly dangerous to it. At the time I was sacked, I was told
that nothing they had found out about me would ever leave the Bank.
I did not believe it at the time but when I got a job almost immediately
in the Ministry of Information and later in the Ministry of Fuel and Power,
I thought it was true. Such was the Bank's 'code' of behaviour.

I learned quite a few lessons from my experience at the Bank. I realised then that the ruling class really does fear the workers. After all I was
a fairly unimportant person both in the Bank and outside it. Yet they spent
considerable sums of money tracking down my background in order to
find out if I were a Communist. I learnt that the ruling class does not
always stick together: for example the Bank was not prepared to share
its knowledge with other employers. I learnt that the Bank did not, and
probably does not yet, believe that democratic government is a good
method of ruling. They behaved in a thoroughly dictatorial and patriar-
chal manner, dictating what sort of dress we should wear (black, blue
or grey and always a hat); they dictated where and what their employees
should say and, on occasions, what time they should go to bed!

I learned very little in my next job at the Ministry of Information
where I found a job in the reference section, apart from learning that
I was pretty poor at the kind of research we did there. One of the things
I did learn was that it was really difficult to convince people that you are
telling the truth, especially when it seems a bit unlikely. I wanted to get
pregnant but not if it meant I would be sacked so I went to a Mrs Atkins
in Establishment and asked her what the position was. I was of course
not married. She refused to believe that I was hoping to be pregnant and
insisted that I already was. Nothing I could say could convince her I was
telling the truth. She said however whether I was pregnant then or would
be so in the future would not make the Ministry sack me. So we parted
with a handshake and expressions of good wishes. In two months time
I was pregnant. It proved to be a difficult pregnancy and a horrendous
delivery. Being a first timer I was registered at a hospital but was transferred at the last minute to a makeshift nursing home in Hertfordshire
where an inexperienced GP attempted a high forceps delivery after six
days first stage labour. The child lived for only two days. She died from
head injuries caused by slipped forceps. I carry the scars, both physical
and mental to this day.

Devastated by this loss and the dictum from the medics that a pregnancy sooner than eighteen months would be highly inadvisable, my

husband Roland and I adopted a five-week old girl, Carol, who saved my sanity and brought joy and delight to the family.

When the war ended I was still at the Ministry of Information. Gradually I got used to working normal hours, and going to the cinema again, and wearing my best clothes for a party. Most of the rationing went on till well after the fighting was ended and practical things like the road signs, shortage of all kinds of foods, and acute crowding of houses and flats went on for what seemed like ages, even after the war with Japan ended. It seemed that very little changed until one started counting the dead and wounded, not only overall but amongst one's friends and acquaintances. What did change quite quickly was the feeling of unity, the feeling that whatever one did was for the common good. The war had broken down many of the divisive elements of life, replaced the isolation by group feeling. This unity had made many amazing feats possible, some small and some large. It gave people a feeling of achievement and a feeling of personal pride because the opportunity presented itself and they were confident enough to grasp it – which they would not have felt capable of had they been standing alone.

The election of a Labour government in 1945, with a reasonable majority of over 100, gave people a further feeling of achievement. They believed that the promise of a better life made by the politicians when encouraging people to work harder for the war effort would be honoured by the new government. The expectation was that major industries would be nationalised, that housing would be controlled, that education would be vastly improved, that gas and electricity would be nationalised, that there would be a free health service, and that the feeling of unity would be continued in the campaigns to improve life through government intervention.

Many of these things happened and, coupled with the benefit of the welfare state to those disadvantaged groups who needed help – the sick, the disabled, the unemployed, those with children, the aged, and the homeless – life for the majority of the population was much improved. Full employment strengthened the economy and work of the trade unions improved the financial situations of their members. The majority believed we would never return to the days of the dole queue and the hunger marches.

Before there was a shift of opinion in society, I'd been fortunate to have found a job in the Ministry of Fuel and Power and among a few people whose views about how things should be run were very like my own. In addition, it was a proper job which I understood, and I also had the luck to be in the right place at the right time.

DAILY GRAPHIC 1 JAN 1948

Women are the 'stars' in New Year Honours

Countess Mountbatten becomes a Dame Grand Cross of the Order of the British Empire.

Miss Margaret Bondfield, Britain's first woman Cabinet Minister, prominent in trade union movement for more than 40 years—new Companion of Honour.

The Hon. Victoria Sackville - West, novelist and poet, is made a Companion of Honour.

Lady Nye, wife of Sir Archibald Nye, Governor of Madras, receives the Kaisar-i-Hind Gold Medal. Her husband, a former Vice C.I.G.S., becomes G.C.S.I.

Dame Beryl Oliver, now Dame Grand Cross of the British Empire

Awards for people who make the wheels turn

? New Year began with a question mark for the two hundred mining families of Resolveth, Glamorgan. They heard up at the pit—Ynysarwed Colliery—where most of them work, that John Evans, an underground worker, had been awarded the B.E.M.

"And," said a miner, "you only have to go two yards in Resolveth to find a John Evans. There are dozens of them (and most of them

By Graphic Reporter

WOMEN—and the "little people" who, humbly and quietly, make the wheels of Britain go round—are the stars of the New Year Honours.

rm the majority of the 2,500 names in the list . . . men from miners' cottages, farms, the police station and the

and the sciences and not forgotten. But accent is on the

rst woman Cabinet rgaret Bondfield, one-ar draper's assistant. ompanion of Honour

kville-West, authoress d," "The Heir" and similarly honoured. ist-essayist T. S. Eliot nly Order of Merit in

ed £70,000

ears' devotion to Red work brings honour l Carnegy Oliver, who Grand Cross. ting £70,000 in six Savings Movement, itress of Llandrog, ets the B.E.M. "My w £100,000" is her

of Fuel and Power Girl," brilliant hose figures about the and consumption of he to the industry, gets She is a 33-year-old wo girls, Mrs. Nancie cer.

There are 29 Knighthoods. Prominent among them is film-maker Michael Balcon, who gave us such pictures as "San Demetrio, London," "The Good Companions," "Next of Kin" and "The Foreman Went To France."

Atom expert John D. Cockcroft is also knighted. So are Plumbers' Union secretary John Stephenson and Boot and Shoe Union secretary George Chester.

Ex-Flying Squad chief, Superintendent Peter Beveridge, C.I.D., the man whose work brought the conviction of Mrs. Ransome, who killed three women in a lonely cottage, receives the M.B.E.

To radium expert Dr. George Stebbings the honour of a C.B.E.

> Coun. U. B. Walmsley, chairman of Chelsea Savings Committee, who is awarded the M.B.E., is a director of the Daily Graphic and Sunday Graphic, Ltd.

comes too late. He died nine days ago.

Oldest recipient of an honour (O.B.E.) is Canon Aubrey Baxter, Chaplain to Chester Royal Infirmary. He is 80.

● All through last winter's blizzards cheery 49-year-old postman C. Headley John Bear, of Morwenstow, Cornwall, fought his way 20 miles a day across wild country to deliver the letters to the villagers of Welcombe.

Sometimes he got back utterly exhausted. But he always went next day. For five days he was the only postman in the area to get through.

Only when he fell on the ice and was injured did he give up.

To-day he receives the B.E.M.

HOME RAIL SALES

By A City Correspondent

SHORTAGE of stock combined with further big reinvestment from final sales of Home Rails accelerated the Industrial upswing in yesterday's Stock Markets.

Once again buying was indiscriminate, the view having gained ground

---

E. Standard Jan 1 1948

Mother-statistician gets 1948 OBE

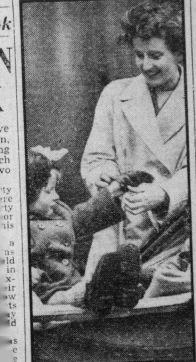

Ministry of Fuel statistician and mother of two children, Mrs. Nancie Elizabeth Berger gets the OBE in the New Year honours. She is seen with daughter Carol in London to-day.

fight

the crisis

with

The winter of 1946-47 was one of the worst on official records. Temperatures plummeted. Roads were blocked with snow and ice. Trains ceased to run and there was an acute shortage of coal both for industry and the domestic market partly due to miners being unable to work, and the lack of transport. As a result, factories stopped working and on the household front people died from hypothermia. Coal was stockpiled at pit heads, and mine owners stopped coal fom coming to the surface because it was cheaper than stockpiling. In the Ministry of Fuel and Power there was chaos. Coal production was still in private hands, though nationalisation was being negotiated, and the Ministry had responsibilities but very limited power.

The Statistical Department of the Ministry of Fuel and Power was divided into two parts: one part dealt with the production statistics – output per man shift, etc. – and the other with consumption statistics. In normal times the production of coal was the important statistic to be watched with the basic figures of: output per man shift, absenteeism, and pit-head stocks. High-flying statisticians worked on these figures helping to make an impact on the amount of coal brought to the surface. At that point their interest waned. This happened mainly because the supply of coal normally was equal to the demand. There were shortages of certain grades such as good house coal, coal for coking ovens, and of course in times of high demand stocks both at pit heads and in all commercial premises were used up. But except in spells of unusually cold weather – or intense industrial activity – consumption of coal was not an 'interesting' field of research. It was a field left to the also-rans, of which I was one.

By February 1947, crisis point had been reached. One Sunday, barely five months after my second child, Vicki, was born, I was called back to the Ministry to help in the crisis. The following days at the Ministry were horrific. A sort of coal rationing scheme was being put together which altered from day to day as high-up officials thought up a daily idea for protecting the big at the expense of the small. The whole scheme was quite unworkable for a number of reasons. First, only coal was to be rationed. The supply of oil, gas, electricity and other fuels – such as coke – were to be 'free', which actually meant that their supply was subject to the effect of the widespread electricity cuts, or reduction of pressure, so far as gas was concerned, and by random cuts to deliveries as far as oil was concerned.

I remember on one occasion when Huge Gaitskill, junior minister to Emmanuel Shinwell, Minister of Fuel and Power, who was chairing a meeting of ministers with interests in the coal supply, asked what happened if a full coal ration to a factory was not delivered in any one week. How was the deficit made up and when? He was amazed to find out that it never was. He had completely failed to understand the rationing scheme, assuming that the 'rationing' of coal was just like the rationing of food.

It became clear by late March that whilst output per man shift was important, production was less crucial than distribution. The ability to spread out coal from the pitheads where it could accessed was more important than the production of a constant supply. This was the area in which I was supposed to be the specialist. I wasn't but I could see the practical possibilities. I also realised that it was important to keep one eye on the views and activities of the newly appointed under-secretary in charge, Francis Hemming, whose reputation as a high-flying civil servant was rivalled only by his reputation as one of the world's experts on the nomenclature of butterflies and moths. It was not long before I realised that Francis, acknowledging his ignorance about fuel supplies, had also decided to keep at least one eye on me.

Together we struggled with the problem. In fact, we had only one option. Unable to apply theories of statistics to the problem because we had little skill in statistics of any kind, we devised methods of numerate presentation based on common sense whose results did not come out too badly. I was by now a sort of protégé of Francis Hemming, though strictly speaking I should have worked with the assistant secretary, who headed -up his department. But Francis always did things the wrong way and in addition he needed someone constantly at his beck and call who held to the same ideas about how to solve crises as he did. So, all my directions came from Francis. He was an amusing companion and though his unorthodox method of working – leaving the office at 5 pm and returning to work at 8 pm generally in the house of one or other of his protégés – led him into trouble. You could rely on his abilities to extricate himself even if you couldn't rely on him to get *you* out of trouble.

Because of Francis's attitude to work, I was in contact with people on a much higher grade than myself. I attended meetings with the Minister, Manny Shinwell, with his permanent secretary, Sir Donald Henderson, with Hugh Gaitskill, as well as a number of highly placed civil servants from my own ministry, and from others who invested in the affairs of coal users.

At that time, just before nationalisation of the mines, the leading district in the country was the Midland Amalgamated District (MAD) and I had the nous to make a friend of the chief executive, Mr Moffatt. He and his colleagues made the running in coal production. Meetings with Moffatt became not so much a discussion on how the coal could best be distributed but rather a battle of wills between the Ministry, represented by myself, and him. Production in the district was high and stocks were at a reasonable level and far better than the rest of the country. I wanted them to distribute coal above their normal levels to supply less well-off districts. Moffatt was against such a move although he knew perfectly well that in was in the best interests of the country to distribute his coal around a bit more. We had a battle of wills, and in the end Moffatt gracefully agreed to a limited 'export' above the normal level, to ease the crisis.

As time went on, distributing the coal that was stockpiled became more difficult. Stocks themselves were depleted, and factories and firms were now living day to day. This meant more work for me but also more interest. I made it my business to be better informed than other ministry officials by keeping in close touch with the district officials in mining areas and then feeding this information to Francis Hemming so that he, in turn, became the best informed senior ministry official.

One day Francis called me into the office and said, 'They want to offer you an MBE,' adding, 'You don't want that do you?' I really had no idea what he was talking about but he went on to explain. 'People in your grade when offered an honour are generally offered an MBE. That's the drill. But you don't want that. You want an O at the least.' It sounded like mumbo-jumbo but I assumed that Francis, who had a string of honours, presumably knew what he was talking about. 'Well, that's what we'll go for,' he said. 'I'll tell them you'll refuse an M but accept an O.' Later, as a result of Francis's homilies on never taking what you are offered, I got the hang of it. Go for the next step up. After that I always did!

The reason I accepted an honour at all was a piece of rationalisation on my part which I thought was justified. Up until then I had managed to get jobs without having to show any paper qualifications. It was lucky I wasn't asked to compete because I had no qualifications whatsoever. I came from a family which considered education for girls a waste of resources. As time went on I knew it would become harder to operate without paper backing and since a degree was something I could neither afford nor aspire to, an honour would be a not so bad alternative.

Francis was right. The sort of people who were awarded MBEs were not those who could be termed high fliers. OBEs were the first range in the professional ladder. Fortunately, I did not have to endure the horror of going to Buckingham Palace to be decorated. During wartime and for a long period afterwards, honours came by post. Although I was spared the hypocrisy of bowing to George VI, I did not escape publicity. I was young and I had two young children, and the papers saw a story in that. As for my colleagues who were political, they criticised me for accepting honours from the enemy – even asking me if OBE stood for 'other bugger's energy'. My less supportive friends asked me why I should get an honour whilst the country suffered from the coal shortage. At least my mother was pleased, even though she was short of coal.

As coal production increased and the cold winter months were replaced by April's spring the emphasis on statistics of coal consumption declined. My importance in the department also declined. Francis and I still had our lunch together (his left arm and hand were nearly useless as a result of a war wound and he needed help to cut up his food) but our evening work sessions ceased. The crisis was over and I went back to the ranks, so to speak. But while it lasted it was interesting and educational.

By the early 1950s the euphoric feelings of the immediate post-war years had begun to fray at the edges and the feeling of unity and togetherness began to crack. When the Tories won the 1951 election, the idea that peace was worth working for and winning was abandoned by everyone apart from the Communist Party. Class differences which had been smothered during the war became even more apparent, as the rich continued to profit from peace as they had done from the war. The less well-off and the downright poor began to feel the pinch. Women who had gained a lot during the war suffered especially. Men returning from the war wanted their jobs back, and the government was happy to go along with the idea that women's place was back in the home, if not in the wrong.

Gradually the Communist Party began to be isolated again. The idea of a common good began to vanish into the air as something we would never grasp firmly again. This question of isolation was probably more marked among those of the political left. Before the war we had been isolated because of our views; during the war our views and opinions gained ground; but a few years after the war the views of the majority slipped back. 'Looking after number one', and the beginning of 'all-right-Jackism' became apparent.

M. B. Jasnogórska (w oryginale)

IX
A Year in Warsaw

gave the children an ice cream & came home & put them to bed. Ro tried to take some the exposures of his children asleep but I doubt if it will come out. Tomorrow we [illegible] letters to Warsaw.

Uneventful car ride to Warsaw through fairly dullish county. Stopped off at Chestakova.? to look at a famous church Jasna Góra where there is the Black Madonna. The church chx chronous, a monument on the rampart of the ancient stronghold, & is very beautiful & impressive standing on a hillock. Pilgrimages are made for all over Poland to this place by cripples & others seeking cure & salvation. The Church itself is immensely ornate

111a

Original in PF.42802
Copies in PF.52673
          SF.411/Poland
Copy for Mr. A. S. Halford, F.O.

Held RS.

4th March, 1949.

PF.42802/B.1.a./HMG.

Dear

Roland and Nancy BERGER.

Roland BERGER and his wife Nancy left the U.K. at the beginning of February 1949 for Warsaw where he has a job as Social Affairs Officer for the United Nations Organization. They are expected to remain in Warsaw for at least a year. Both are long-standing members of the British Communist Party, having been connected during the 1939 - 1945 war with some of its under cover groups.

Roland BERGER was born on 18th December, 1904, and is the owner of British Passport No. 0.260439 issued in Warsaw on 22nd April, 1948. He also holds United Nations Laissez-Passer No. 0674, valid from 5.2.48 to 5.2.49.

Nancy BERGER was born on 8th March, 1914 and is the owner of British Passport No.1098911 issued in London on 3rd January, 1949.

Yours sincerely,

H. M. Gee.

S. I. S.

IN FEBRUARY 1949 the whole family took off for Poland, Roland and Carol sailing on the MS *Batory*, a Polish ship, whilst Vicki and I travelled by air to Copenhagen. There we boarded the *Batory* and sailed together to Gdynia in the north of Poland. When we arrived we got into the oldest car I have ever travelled in and headed for the seaside resort of Sopot and what seemed to me to be a very posh hotel, with two huge bedrooms and a sitting room, where we ate wonderful salmon with all the trimmings at 11 pm. I pondered on what it would be like in a country when I didn't know the language, had no knowledge of the type of food eaten, and where the housing was reputed to be the worst in Europe. Coupled with all this were the rumours of starvation, the horror of the bombed cities and the fact that I knew no one, although Roland had made a few friends. How, I wondered, would I be able to cope properly with two children aged two and four in such a situation?

At breakfast we ordered omelettes. They came and looked beautiful if a bit on the large side. Alas, they were filled with a large amount of strawberry jam. None of us could manage them, so we ordered boiled eggs. These came turned out of their shells into cups. The children rejected them in favour of a piece of bread. It took a long time for us to learn what to order in hotels and restaurants, what the children – who were normally not fussy – would eat.

Rationing, of a kind, was still in operation, but there seemed to be no shortage of food. What I did not realise then was that since Roland worked for United Nations Relief and Rehabilitation Administration and was paid in dollars, we were very privileged because dollars could buy almost anything

When we arrived at our rented apartment in Warsaw we discovered a fish swimming around in the bath. The good news was that a very nice

Polish young woman, Filomena, was installed and willing to stay with us for as long as we wanted her. I wondered about the fish. Filomena said she was waiting for a friend to collect it, and that it was common practice to 'store' fish alive in the bath as at the time refrigeration was almost non-existent for private households. The apartment was pretty scruffy but this was post-war Warsaw, and one didn't grumble, not at first anyway. Subsequently – in about five days – we discovered that we were sharing the apartment with the woman who let it to us, a form of minor cheating on the part of the landladies in Warsaw at the time when accommodation was so scarce that tenants would put up with a lot of inconvenience just to get a roof over their heads. So we moved into a much better flat – the ground floor of a newly built house where the boss of Beton Stal lived in the flat above us. Our street had the wonderful name of Pilota Idzikowskiego and our house was surrounded by a high fence of heavy metal. Entrance was possible only through a small gate operated electronically from inside the flat.

This fencing proved a useful aid to communication for the children. Both of them were shy and language was a problem. At first they communicated with the local children with the fence between them. They felt quite safe. Later when they learned a few words of Polish they felt able to admit one or two children to play with them. Later they would admit a dozen at a time who often ate from our well-stocked larder.

I had been warned that food in Poland was very short and was ready for strict economy and plain meals. Our contacts among embassy staff, both British and American, bought food mainly from the American PX stores. To me it seemed madness to be eating tinned spinach when the fields around the house were sown with first class vegetables and the shops had plenty to sell. Meat was of course the most strictly rationed. Filomena, our great helper, would say 'there is no meat today.' We'll have eggs or vegetables, I would say. 'Oh that's not necessary,' she would state firmly. 'There is pork, chicken, turkey, duck or goose.' To a Pole meat meant beef, and we rarely saw any though people queued for hours to be rewarded with a couple of kilos for each person with a ration book.

Our 'rations' were easily available. Salmon fished from the Vistula river, whether fresh of smoked, was sold at a price which was very reasonable to those with dollars to exchange. We had it often. When we came home to London after a year in Warsaw the children could not understand why smoked salmon was such a luxury. Milk was a bit of a problem. Fresh pasteurised Polish milk was hard to find and anyway, according to World Health Organisation vets in Warsaw, pretty deathly to drink. So we bought it from the American Embassy, going every other day to collect several litres.

It was flown in from Germany. Back in London when the children saw diplomatic cars running around they asked what they were. 'Embassy cars,' I would say. 'Why do we have to have embassies when we've got a milkman?' they wanted to know. I was stumped for an answer. Both children spoke good Polish quickly, and I marvelled at the way they got most of the quite complicated grammar correct. My Polish was strictly kitchen language, and even that was poor. I remember one day being in the kitchen talking to Filomena in what I thought was Polish in front of a woman trader who came to our door offering veal. When I left the room the women trader said to Filomena, 'I did not know you understood English.'

Life in Poland was nothing like as difficult as I expected it would be. Our new apartment was very spacious and well furnished. Upstairs lived the owners, the Szypkowskis, a family of four, and in the basement lived the caretaker with his ten year old daughter. The children very quickly developed relationships with both families. As is usual with Polish families, meals consisted of a light breakfast on rising – a beverage and perhaps a piece of bread. Then a second breakfast – *drugie śniadanie* – was taken at about 10am, at the house or at work for those employed – and a lunch at about 3pm at the end of the working day which had started at around 7am. A light snack was taken at around 9pm.

The children soon saw possibilities for them in having two regimes. They had breakfast with Roland and me before he went to work, another with Szypkowskis at 10 am, lunch with me at 1pm and if they felt in need of further nourishment another meal with Szypkowskis at around 3pm. However many foods were totally unobtainable such as citrus fruits, bananas, and other foreign fruits. I remember when we were invited to a party at the British embassy a day or two after the Ambassador had paid a visit to the Soviet Union. He had brought back a present for the Poles, a consignment of oranges. Guests at the party took home as many as they could carry. The next day oranges were on sale by itinerant traders, on Marszałkowska.

As foreigners with dollars we lived a very different life from the Poles themselves. Housing was short and any available living space was crammed full. One evening we went to dinner at the home of a high placed government official. We were seated on what we thought was a rather high bench-seat against the wall. After a little time I realised that we were sitting on their bed. The table in front of us and the two chairs on the other side took up the other space in the room. The kitchen was in a cupboard and there was no bathroom. The lavatory was outside. That was good accommodation in Warsaw in 1949. Some people were living in flats and homes which, as a result of the war, had no windows and no facilities

at all. But the cheerfulness of the population seemed to overcome these difficulties, and I used to marvel at the men and women who emerged from among the ruins looking well turned out and ready for work.

The winter weather conditions were hard to cope with. It was just not possible to go out without a hat and gloves, and it was best to cover one's legs with a long coat and high boots, though even the bits between got chapped. Moisture in the nose froze, and so did the inside of windows. I remember our friend Dr Winnicka, who worked with Roland and became our 'adviser', forbade me to open windows in the winter. 'Many people die from frost bite but few from foul air,' she liked to say.

Even in the winter Poles worked long, hard hours. In the winter it was possible to see men and women working on the scaffolding of buildings with bottles of vodka tied round their waists, drunk to stave off the extreme cold.

We travelled a lot around the country, partly on Roland's official business as a social service UNRRA adviser and partly for interest and pleasure. After a holiday in Wisła on the Czech border where the landscape was fresh and beautiful and the town was prosperous and well kept, we journeyed to *Oświęcim* (Auschwitz). The actual town of Oświęcim was pretty dreary with many block-like 'buildings' and a myriad of railway sidings and marshalling yards. Its easy access from both east and west was the main reason the Germans chose it for the concentration camp.

Our visit to Oświęcim was part of a tour to the western side of Poland and included Poznań which is the first town we had visited which was previously German. The population of Poznań was moved in after the Germans were evacuated. Imagine a town the size of Leeds being cleared and entirely repopulated in less than five years. The streets there were wide, the buildings very solid looking, and it did not have the lightness of touch that other Polish cities had. There was no sign of war damage, and the German influence of orderliness was very evident. We also noticed that the state shops were bigger than those in Warsaw and the people better dressed.

There was a trade fair going on when we were there with pavilions from many countries. The Soviet pavilion held the central position and was topped with hundreds of red flags flying in the breeze. Exhibits there included cars, tractors, aeroplanes, bulldozers, and cranes as well as furs, wine, cigarettes, and many varieties of food, canned and in glass jars. Many other countries, including Britain, exhibited in Poznań. We spent some time at the United Nations exhibit where Roland attracted quite a crowd by writing down an address for information in his notebook and giving it to an enquiring student. This started quite a demand for similar information and a queue formed which lasted about twenty minutes. Previously little interest had been shown in this exhibition!

Our visit to the concentration camp at Oświęcim and the extension Birkenau started with a talk from an ex-inmate, a Jewish Pole, as he steered us through the archway of iron which bore the slogan *Arbeit Macht Frei* – Work Sets you Free. What we were entering was in fact a museum which used to be the central part of the camp. This was surrounded by two electrified fences, about five yards apart, making two circles. The area between the fences was floodlit illuminating an area covered with rows and rows of one-storey brick buildings, most housing the exhibits of the museum but some still housing a few German prisoners of war. As we passed one building a Polish soldier rang a bell and these prisoners fell into line and marched off for their lunch. A dejected lot they looked. One wanted to spit on them.

The exhibits in the buildings were a variety of possessions of those who went to the gas chambers. Not a few pairs of spectacles but thousands of them; not one baby's bottle but hundreds. Not one handbag but thousands. Hundreds of knapsacks, some with names on them, stuffed with clothes and toilet things piled up in the corner, piles of human hair taken from the dead bodies after they came from the gas chambers. On the walls are pictures of larger things, sewing machines, prams, stoves.

132

133

The people were told they were going to a better life and chose to bring possessions which would be useful to them.

In these buildings too are the punishment cells: the beating blocks, the solitary confinement blocks, the hanging gibbets, the 'confinement cells' where twenty-five men and women were forced into about twenty-five square feet of space with only one small window. In one confinement cell there were two pictures etched into the plaster by a fingernail. Today they are covered with a glass shield. These were bad enough but the 'cabinet' – built like an oven with a bottom drawer and about two feet square, into which four men were put to stand for days on end, was a sight one could hardly bear to look at.

The reconstruction of the gas chamber was a ghastly sight. There were hundreds of thousands of empty cans which contained the Cyclon B gas used to killed the inmates of the camp. Each can of Cyclon B could kill 20,000 people. Each inmate had clutched a numbered stone which looked like a piece of soap. They thought they were going for a bath.

The commander of the Oświęcim camp, Rudolf Höss, had been associated with the management of concentration camps since 1934 and reached the highest post when he became commander of Auschwitz in 1940. When he testified before the International Tribunal on 5 April 1946 he revealed the extraordinary Nazi bestiality.

'I commanded Auschwitz from May 1940 until 1 December 1943 and estimate that at least 2,500,000 victims were executed and exterminated there by gassing and burning, at least another half a million succumbed to starvation and disease, making a death total of 3,000,000. The figure represents about seventy or eighty per cent of all persons sent to Auschwitz as prisoners, the remainder having been selected and used for slave labour in concentration camp industries. Among the executed and burned were approximately 20,000 Russian prisoners of war who were delivered at Auschwitz in Wehrmacht transports. The remainder included 100,000 German Jews and a great number of citizens, mostly Jewish, from Holland, France, Belgium, Poland, Hungary, Czechoslovakia, Greece or other countries. We executed about 400,000 Hungarian Jews alone at Auschwitz in the summer of 1944. When I set up the extermination building in Auschwitz, I used Cyclon B, which we dropped into the death chamber through a small opening. It took from three to fifteen minutes to kill the people, depending on climactic conditions. We knew when the people were dead because their screaming stopped. We usually waited about half an hour before we opened the doors and removed the bodies. After the bodies were removed, our special commandos took off the rings and extracted the gold from the teeth of the corpses.

'Another improvement we made over Treblinka was that we built our gas chambers to accommodate 2,000 people at one time, whereas at Treblinka their ten gas chambers accommodated only 200 people each… Children of tender ages were invariably exterminated since they were unable to work. We made still another improvement over Treblinka. At Treblinka the victims almost always knew that they were to be executed. At Auschwitz we endeavoured to fool the victims into thinking that they were to go through a delousing process. Of course frequently they realised our true intentions, and we sometimes had riots and difficulties as a consequence. Frequently women would hide their children under their clothes, but, of course, when we found that out we would send the children to be exterminated. We were required to carry out these

exterminations in secrecy but, of course, the foul and nauseating stench from the continuous burning of bodies permeated the entire area, and all of the people living in the surrounding communities knew what exterminations were going on at Auschwitz.'

Höss was by no means an unusual specimen of Nazi bestiality. He had been brought up a devout Catholic. There was nothing in his past to make him a criminal. He gave his testimony in a cold-blooded, unemotional voice. Without even a flicker of remorse, he related how, to save time and gas, Jewish children were thrown alive in the ovens during the 1944 'rush season'. He explained that in the Summer of 1941, Himmler called for him and ordered the final solution (Endloesung) of the Jewish question. He added coldly that he selected Auschwitz because of convenient transportation facilities and remoteness.

Birkenau, a camp for women and an extension of Oświęcim, was, if that is possible, more horrifying than the main camp. Nothing had been tidied up, the huts where the inmates lived were the same as they were when in use, the walls were marked where the lice had been squashed. These barracks were filled with thin plank shelves where inmates spent their time, eating and sleeping as well as other activities to pass the time. There was absolutely no sanitation, no water, light only through windows in the roof. To see how the people lived was so real that it produced a sort of sickness which lasted with me for twenty-four hours during which I was unable to eat. My husband was affected in the same way. Fortunately we had not taken the children into the camps although we did explain to them what the camps were built for.

Over the whole camp had hung a terrible though indistinct smell. It seemed to cling to one's clothes and skin and was difficult to get rid of. It was not a pungent smell but sometimes it comes back to me even now. Then I crave for clean water, clean clothes and a clean bed.

On our way back to Warsaw we called in at Częstochowa to look at the famous church Jasna Góra where there is a picture of Czarny Madonna (the Black Madonna of Częstochowa). We saw also the huge ornate church; a monument on the ramparts of an ancient stronghold. Pilgrimages are made from all over Poland to this church, which has the reputation of curing the disabled and other invalids. It is rather like Lourdes in France, with crutches, wheelchairs, sticks, stretchers, etc., piled up near the church, discarded by the people who had been cured. I found this place rather revolting with men and women kissing the floor and the feet of statues. We stood at the doorway of one of the chapels watching the service. At one point we heard the 'trumpets of heaven' coupled with a terrific rumbling – presumably the rumblings of heaven or hell. The Catholics at Jasna Góra certainly knew how to put on a show. All I could think of was that Rudolf Höss, commander of Oświęcim, was said to be a devout Catholic.

The Czarny Madonna was to gain more publicity at a later stage of our stay in Poland. One day the newspapers reported that she was crying tears of blood because of the wickedness of the Polish Communist government. The time was the end of June, during the middle of the harvest.

Hundreds of thousands flocked to Częstochowa by train, by cart, by motorcar, by bicycle, and on their feet. Communications were in chaos. Trucks moving the grain from the fields to the processing mills were blocked by the traffic. That part of the country was disrupted at a time when only efficiency would get the harvest under cover.

I could scarcely imagine that people would believe the 'tears of blood' story. So I consulted a Roman Catholic friend of mine, a scientist whose views I respected. To my amazement he said he believed in what was 'happening'. When I suggested that it was a trick of the reactionaries in the church who were trying to disrupt the harvest, cause food shortages, and damage the record of the government, my scientist friend would have none of this. The tears of blood were genuine he asserted. It was no use arguing.

The crowds going to Częstochowa continued to increase, whilst the government put out feeble pleas for people to stay at home. No direct attack was made on the church. At that same time it was too strong to argue with.

The end came suddenly. After a week when the crowds were already causing injuries a young girl was crushed to death in the crowd before the portrait. The government finally acted, trains to the area were cancelled, and roads were blocked off. The Roman Catholic Church realised it had bitten off more than it could chew and joined the Government's plea for people to remain at home.

One of the excitements in Warsaw at this time was the building of the east-west track (the Trasa Voset) – a major thoroughfare across the city. The tunnel went under Novy Swiat, one of the main roads in the city. 10,000 men and women were working on the project which included a long escalator sent from the Soviet Union. It was the only escalator in Warsaw and was quickly working and swarmed on every day by hundreds of people just going for the ride on this great novelty. We paid a visit at night and it looked like a Hollywood movie set as we looked towards the tunnel from the riverside. We missed the official opening on 22 July 1950 as we went on our summer holiday to France and then England.

Returning to Warsaw after the summer break I made up my mind that after I had completed a year in Poland I would need to return to London and stop there. Some people can flit around the world making hundreds of contacts but no real friends. Roland could operate that way but I could not. I needed real friends who could be supportive and need the kind of support I could give.

I've learned a lot since I was there. It had been hard but rewarding. A major lesson had been how hard it is to build socialism. I try to apply the situation there to the one we might have in Britain. The Poles, of course, had the Soviet Union base to help them. Some used to say that to have one's socialism given by another country or the army of another country is a major disadvantage, and I would agree. Millions of Poles don't know what socialism is – it all came too suddenly with no fight to consolidate the people and no real need to solve the big problems because the Soviet Union with its great strength and influence will do it for you. But at a price and that price is dependence of a kind that takes the initiative and fight out of the majority of the people. The leaders, the activists may benefit from this dependence – it gives them assistance, advice and resources. The real victims of the system are the real dependents – the mass of the people who don't really know what is going on because they are not involved. When things get bad they start attacking those on whom they are dependent, not knowing how much worse it would be if their 'patron' were not behind them.

The last few months in Poland were somewhat grim. The anti-foreigner era was beginning, and trials of so-called spies from the West were being held in the Soviet Union and elsewhere in the eastern block. The atmosphere had a devastating effect on those of our Polish friends who visited us regularly. They began to fade away either saying they were too busy or just not turning up. It was some time before we cottoned on to the fact that they were afraid of being accused of using social occasions to pass over information and spying for the West. A few defied the atmosphere and continued to come to see us. One was Dr Makower, an outstanding person. He and his wife had been taken to the Warsaw Ghetto in 1941 and made three attempts to escape, narrowly escaping being shot on two occasions. When finally successful, they both hid for eighteen months in a tiny room in a small village, never going out in daylight.

One great treat we had in Warsaw was to hear Paul Robeson singing to ten thousand people, most of whom had never seen a black man before. They applauded him until their hands were tired. He sang some classical songs loved by the Poles and some Russian songs and his old favourites. The one the audience seemed to like best was *Ma Curly-Headed Baby*.

STARANIEM KOMISJI CENTRALNEJ ZWIĄZKÓW ZAWODOWYCH

KORT CENTRALNY W. K. S. „LEGIA"
— Warszawa —
Środa, 1. VI. 49 r. Godz. 19⁰⁰

PAUL
ROBESON

Przy fortepianie: BRUNO RAIKIN

z udziałem

Chóru i Orkiestry Polskiego Radia
pod dyr. JERZEGO KOŁACZKOWSKIEGO

Cena programu zł 10.—

X
A Job and International Solidarity

141

Demands, needs or rights?

Gaol me, says mother

An appeal by a mother of five to be allowed to go to prison " for a rest " was granted by Southend magistrates yesterday.

Mrs Winifred Gourlay (28), was sentenced to one month after she admitted stealing a child's tricycle, valued at £16, and unlawfully selling it. A six-month suspended sentence for an earlier theft was brought into effect, to run consecutively. Mrs Gourlay, of Grove Road, Southend, had four previous convictions.

Mr H. Maxwell Lewis, defending, said : " The world has got on top of her. She feels prison would give her a rest from the struggle of feeding and clothing the family and finding the rent money." Mrs Gourlay received £22 in Social Security.

WE LEFT POLAND IN the Spring of 1950. It was bitterly cold and snowy. We travelled by train to Paris after stopping off at Prague. It was so cold that we hired a room in a hotel in which to spend the five hours we had to wait for the train to Paris. Luckily, we had a plastic box full of curried chicken left over from a feast we had eaten the night before. At 11 am we ate it and nothing ever tasted as good.

Back in London my main concern was to find a job. I was faced again with my lack of qualifications so I plumped for a job as a freelance journalist. I had some experience from before the war, editing the *Holborn Outlook* – a monthly paper published jointly by the Communist and Labour Parties. Patrick Monkhouse, a leader writer on the *Evening Standard* and a member of the editorial board of the *Outlook*, had given me some training that now stood me in good stead, and I started working for technical papers in the building and construction industry and on safety issues in industrial sites. Alongside my journalistic work I was the General Secretary of the Institute of Certified Ambulance Personnel, a body promoting training for ambulance workers and organising examinations. I managed to scratch a living until, by a lucky break, I got the editorship of a magazine covering welfare catering including school meals. This move led me into a field which occupied the rest of my working career.

Politically, I had become active in other organisations including the National Assembly of Women (NAW), a left-wing organisation which tried to involve women in political matters. It was affiliated with the Women's International Democratic Federation, an organisation with membership in many countries including China and the Soviet Union. In 1960, I represented the Assembly at a delegate meeting in East Berlin.

The major women leaders of Russia and of China were present, and their presence made it clear that the meeting had an importance greater than indicated by the agenda. The attitude of both the Russians and the Chinese towards the delegation from the major countries was such that I began to realise we were being wooed. It was not until I heard the word revisionism that I realised we were being asked to stand up and be counted in the arguments between the two countries.

The arguments were of a fundamental nature. The Chinese Communist Party (CCP) was accusing the Russian Communist Party (CPSU) of departing from the principals of Marxism-Leninism in the development of their country, a departure which they characterised as revisionism, a road they said was towards capitalism.

The differences between the two countries led to a political split and to withdrawal from the two countries of diplomatic personnel and technical advisers. The Chinese were especially angry about the withdrawal of Russian technical advisers of which there were many in China as they depended on them for the skills needed for the construction of many types of industrial buildings such as glass making, chemicals and engineering products. When I discussed these withdrawals with comrades in China in 1963 they were almost tearful about the matter because they had made good friends of the Russian advisers, who incidentally had taken away every bit of documentation along with the blueprints of the projects they were helping with.

The NAW was also connected to organisations in South Africa. In October 1962 the world was shocked by the news that Helen Joseph, an activist in the anti-apartheid struggle, had been placed under house arrest in Johannesburg. The shock was not so much that a South African citizen should be confined but that a white woman was the first to suffer this punishment at the hands of the Prime Minister Verwoerd under the new Sabotage Act. In 1961 she had been acquitted from charges of high treason in the mammoth Treason Trial and had immediately arranged and commenced a tour of the country, visiting banished people and making contact with the various units of the Federation of South African Women (FSAW) of which she was the General Secretary. Before she left she had arranged for me to join her on the trip, meeting in Durban. I was sponsored by the Women's International Democratic Federation to which the Womens' Assembly was affiliated.

Helen knew South Africa well, having lived there since 1931, when she arrived from India to take up a teaching post in a private school in Durban. She had no perception of the depth of the racist policies of the nationalist government when she arrive, but as she became involved in the struggle she became a steadfast fighter for equal rights and a brave and courageous opponent of the government's apartheid policies. She had survived five years of the 1956 Treason Trial travelling from Johannesburg to Pretoria every day, often transporting other defendants, including Nelson Mandela. She was a first class organiser, made an outstanding job of coordinating the Federation of South African Women and threw herself entirely into work for the non-whites of the country.

Though she lacked a full and deep political understanding of the struggle in South Africa and the rest of the world, in a sense this was one of her strengths. No one could accuse her of acting on the orders of any party or organisation. No one could call her a Communist. She acted from the heart, and everything she did was sincere and with one aim in hand – to gain a better life for the non-whites of South Africa. As such she stood shoulder to shoulder with such women leaders as Violet Weinberg, Lilian Nygoyi, Molly Fischer, Ray Alexander, Dora Tomana, Elizabeth Mafeking, and Sophie Williams, to name a few. One of her triumphs had been the organisation of the women's demonstration in Pretoria in 1956. 2,000 women, white and non-white, by one means or another, each holding their own signed petition, had gathered in the front of the Union Building in the city. They took the authorities by surprise on this occasion and decided to organise another day in Pretoria. This time, in excess of 20,000 came, arriving in Pretoria by bus but walking to the Union building in groups of not more than three so that they would not be arrested for unlawful assembly.

When I arrived in Johannesburg Helen had actually set off. She didn't wait for me because she was afraid that the authorities would clamp another confinement order on her. I spent a few days in Johannesburg with Violet Weinburg, Molly Fischer, and Hilda Bernstein who took me into the townships where Lilian Nygoyi lived. I still remember the address – 9970 White City, Orlando West. They showed me round the city but best of all they talked to me and explained what was going on in the anti-apartheid movement. They took me to see Alan Paton and told me that conditions were pushing him further towards the left. When I saw him he said, 'When the Sabotage Bill becomes law there will be four options. To leave the country; to shut up and lead a quiet life; to resort to violence; or to resort to sabotage.'

Rowley Arenstein, a lawyer who worked ceaselessly on cases of non-whites in the courts, took me to listen to some cases and explained to me the way the anti-apartheid movement used the courts as part of the struggle.

On 24 May 1962, the three of us – Helen, Joe Morolong and I – started on our tour to track down some of the banished people. Joe was our interpreter and contact man. Many of the people we wished to meet lived in the townships or on state farms, places where white people were not allowed to go. Our technique was to drop Joe off near to the place we could contact our banished person. He would arrange the time we should return in the darkness. Our first contact was Kenneth Morenyi at Tugela Ferry. He was banished after police shootings in Zeernat which followed

" And what did you really want to do, Sir ? "

the refusal of the women there to accept passes. Our meeting took place at the roadside with Kenneth acting like he was serving tea to two white ladies. Joe kept watch and both he and Kenneth disappeared into the bushes if suspicious cars came into view. Kenneth had taken a correspondence course in building and earned a few pounds mending roofs and such. He was under constant pressure from the authorities to sign a statement asking for his release. Of course the statement also contained a clause saying he would not engage in any political activity when he got home. He refused to sign on many occasions. He wanted only one thing from us. Did his name still stand high with Congress?

We pressed on from one banished person to another, some living in half a tin hut with only two pounds a month from the government and a few rands the movement sent them. Once we got into a reserve as it looked like a good way through to where we wanted to go but it turned out to be a really rough road and we actually had to get out of the car and move the rocks before we could proceed. Helen, who had been arrested in a reserve two weeks previously and fined twenty rand by the magistrate was quite alarmed that she would not fare so well at the next arrest and was also upset at the thought of me being arrested and probably deported. We arrived in King Williams Town when it was still light so we had to walk around until it was dark enough to crawl in a rondavel on a Trust Farm which was the home of a banished man. When our eyes became accustomed to the semi-darkness – the only light was from two candles – we saw that the rondavel was 'furnished' with one bed with a mattress, one mattress on the floor, one chair, a primus stove, a cooking stove and nothing else. Absolutely nothing else. Here we met a young man who had been swindled out his chieftainship and his mother whose husband had been murdered by the Special Branch.

Our next stop was Port Elizabeth. It was a public holiday and the executive of the local Food and Canning Workers Union was having a meeting so we stopped off to greet them, and they interrupted their business to greet us. This was a very strong union, with both Black and Coloured workers in it.* As we went into the room they all gave us the Congress 'thumbs up' sign.

In the evening we attended a meeting of the Executive of the Port Elizabeth branch of the FSAW where both Helen and I spoke. At this meeting we discussed the possibility of a public meeting at which we should both speak but decided against it as it would most certainly have attracted the attention of the police and we ran the risk of bringing our

* Coloured, and various sub-groups, was the given political categorisation of people of mixed race, by the apartheid National government.

tour to a premature end. Instead we decided to have a meeting of representatives from all the clubs in the Federation.

The meeting took place in an African household situated in the township of New Brighton, and we were conveyed by car and asked to cover our heads so that headlights of other cars would not show up our white faces. At this meeting Florence Motomela was present. At that time she was confined to the isolated and small township of New Brighton under a five year banning order. Her position was similar to that of Lilian Nygoyi but at least she was in the very centre of a well organised Congress Alliance community. Florence was a courageous and charming woman. In her speech she said, 'Never mind the winds and the rains. We will fight. We are working for our children's future. Tomorrow is not ours because we do not know what will happen. The little difficulties we have will pass over. Tomorrow we will have the new ideas which must exist in every woman's heart. As I am sitting here there are 'Nats'* all over me. But if my comrades are with me five years will seem like five days. I will help all I can and hope it is the same with Lilian. I feel deeply for her and I send her my greetings. When I think about the Sabotage Bill I want to tear my clothes in anger. It is better to kill us than for us to knuckle under this Bill. But we will find loopholes. We shall win eventually. Make no mistake, you will see us one day in London. And you will be at the airport. Please be on time!'

The meeting of the representatives of the clubs on Saturday afternoon turned out to be one hundred strong. Most of the women turned up in their black and green Federation blouses, and as Helen and I walked into the hall with the Chair they started to sing. The singing went on until everyone was seated, and the Chair then said a short prayer, and a hymn was sung. She then made a speech asking all those present to voice their problems so that Helen Joseph as General Secretary could answer them in her speech. Many spoke.

I was then introduced with a build-up greater than I deserved but, I was to her, and to all of them, a representative of the WIDF, a worldwide organisation of women like themselves, and as such they honoured me. I spoke to them about the struggles of women in my country and in other countries of the world. I told them about the anti-apartheid campaigns in Britain and about the boycott. I spoke to them as a comrade and a friend deeply interested in all they were doing and tried to indicate to them the respect and admiration the women of other countries had for the struggle that they themselves were putting up against such tremendous odds.

* The Nationalist Party

REPORT ON A VISIT TO SOUTH AFRICA
SPONSORED BY THE WOMEN'S INTERNATIONAL
DEMOCRATIC FEDERATION

May 16 - June 10, 1962

----

* While the whole of this Report is not confidential
there are certain sections of it which are. In
the event of a circulation wider than executive
committee of the WIDF reference should be made to
the writer.

NAN BERGER

Thank you for being a friend of freedom.

Oliver Tambo
President

Nelson Mandela
Deputy President

At the end of my speech they applauded with great enthusiasm. For them it was a great occasion to meet someone from Britain who was sympathetic towards them and understood their problems. One woman in African tribal dress rose to her feet and said, 'I have not seen a woman from overseas before, and now I have seen one I feel more free. I feel I have seen everything. I have now seen the spirit of Mandela. It is among us in the person of Nan.'

It was about the biggest tribute which she could have paid to the WIDF and I felt very proud to be the subject of such deep appreciation.

One after another the women got up and referred to the 'spirit of Mandela among us' and thanked me for being there and the WIDF for sending me. Then it was announced that they would like to sing a song in my honour and they sung a song in Sesutho that was about Nelson Mandela, the words of which are, 'Here cometh Mandela. He is with power. Come ye all. Let us build together.'

At the end of the meeting everyone danced a sort of township jazz step and they were delighted that I danced with them. By this time the meeting was in a state of great enthusiasm and someone suggested that the next congress of FSAW should have representation from every country in the world. Everyone agreed and someone shouted out 'And Nan shall come from her country.' At once the whole room full of people took up the chant 'We want Nan. We want Nan.' Such treatment from such courageous and warm-hearted people makes one very proud of what one represents, and it has the effect of making one feel that with their support one could move mountains. I came away from the meeting much strengthened in my political resolution.

If I were the spirit of Mandela to them, they were the spirit of the working class to me.

The women of Port Elizabeth are great fighters and one of the weapons they used was the boycott. If traders and factories behaved in a way to which they take exception they applied the boycott and in almost all cases the boycott was successful. On one occasion a dry-cleaning works had come under boycott, and in a few weeks it was practically out of business. The owners came to the Congress Alliance and said they would mend their ways if the boycott could be called off. The women said they would be glad to call it off but had no money to send out notices. The owners said they would provide money for a circular. A four-page bulletin was prepared giving all the congress news, announcements and news of future activities (including boycotts). The dry-cleaning firm paid and in return they got a one-line note at the end of the bulletin to say that they were no longer the subject of boycott.

By driving hard all day we reached Cape Town in one day, arriving at 11pm. The next morning we had a meeting in our room at 7am to make arrangements for our stay in the city. Throughout our stay our hostess arranged early morning meetings, meetings at meals and meetings in between meals so that none of our time was wasted.

The Congress movement in Cape Town is a very broad movement and the FSAW, as part of it, had helped its success in operating on this very broad front. Before we arrived they had joined with the other women's organisation and called a special church service of protest against the Sabotage Bill and for individual members to act and work with both the Black Sash, a non-violent white women's resistance organisation which operated an office to advance money for bail, and the Quakers' Defence and Aid Committee, which helped those who are politically victimised via the courts.

The burdens which non-whites bear do not make them incapable of enjoying life. Africans have a determination to enjoy their lives whatever the terrors, current and to come, and some of this spontaneous joy rubs off on the more stolid Europeans.

I was surprised at the outspokenness of the English language press. During the time the Sabotage Bill was going through the House of Assembly this section of the press was highly critical of the government. Even at times of lesser tension the English language press has continually criticised the government for its policies on group areas, job registration and Bantu education.

Bantu education was an aspect of apartheid about which not enough is known outside South Africa, and it strikes at the very heart of human dignity. It was education for perpetual servitude. In 1955 the Bantu Education Act came into operation and education for Africans came under the Minister responsible for native affairs and not under the Minister of Education as formerly. Dr Verwoerd said at the time, 'The school must equip him (the native) to meet the demands which the economic life of South Africa will impose upon him... there is no place for the native in European society above the level of certain forms of labour.' It is true that before the Bantu Education Act came into force education for Africans was poor but it existed, and the curriculum followed in African mission schools enabled those who were determined and gifted to progress to white universities. The curriculum in the schools is now debased and includes subjects which show the African that his place is one of servitude. Housecleaning, gardening, etc., are taught as they will be useful to men and women in later life. Academic subjects are pruned away to the basic necessities of reading, writing and arithmetic. Teaching was done in the vernacular in a language where text books were almost non-existent. Bantu education was one of the chief instruments of the government's policy of racialism and it was bitterly opposed by Africans.

One of the trips we made on our journey south was to Basutoland to meet Elizabeth Mafekeng, organiser for the Food and Canning Workers Union in Paarl, Cape, who was banished in 1959 to Vryburg, in the northern Transvaal, a remote place on the edge of the Kalihari desert. The day before the order was to come into operation she fled to Basutoland. Elizabeth was the mother of eleven children, and the many appeals for the Minister of Justice to show some mercy fell on deaf ears. With the support of her friends and comrades who physically shielded her from the police who had got wind of her intention to flee and who tried to stop her going, she was able to get away onto British territory. She told me the story of her flight, and that crowds had surrounded the car which she was to use to prevent the police getting near her. Her child and a suitcase of her clothes were taken in another car, and somewhere on the road to Maseru the two cars met, and she was re-united with her two-month-old baby. Eight miles away from Maseru, at night and in the pitch dark, the car had broken down. Three hours later, the car was moving again, and they entered Basutoland in the early morning, and by mid-morning they had got to Roma where they stopped for food. An hour and a half later students from the Roman Catholic College came to tell her that her flight from South Africa and her description had been announced on the radio and that she was believed to be in Basutoland. She knew that by this time South African special branch would be looking for her and so, with the help of the students, the Basutoland Congress Party, and others, she was hidden until night time and then was taken to the mountains where she climbed for a couple of hours with her child on her back to a remote hiding place.

A TRIP TO CHINA

An illustrated talk by

N A N   B E R G E R,   O. B. E.

13th October at 8 p.m.

A talk in the
"Tuesday Evening" series

Ask at the Library for a bookmark
giving the full programme for the
session

Admission free

St. Pancras Public Libraries

A woman's place . . . in China today it may easily be at the wheel of a man-sized tractor.

LI HAN AND

"THE days when I was just a nobody are not so far behind," said Li Han as she served me tea in her two-room, one-storey house in Wuhan, south-east China.

"Then, if someone knocked on the door when my husband was out and called 'Anyone at home?' I replied 'No' automatically.

"I had no rights as a citizen or a wife. To my husband I was a piece of property. No wonder I was ready to deny my own existence in my own home!"

Dressed in a simple, blue cotton jacket and black trousers, Li—like millions of other Chinese women —wore flat shoes and no make-up. Her hair was pulled straight back into a bun.

"Yes, things have changed in the last ten years," she said. "Come to our factory and see for yourself."

Li's factory is a co-operative workshop. Twenty-five men and 74 women work there. Li is the director, and to watch her at work —using her charm and wit to settle a problem here, and determination and tact to break a production bottleneck there — it seems almost impossible that she learnt to read and write only after the founding of the People's Republic in 1949.

She and seven other women founded the factory because they wanted to take advantage of their new status as housewives. China's new constitution rules that women shall enjoy equal rights with men in all spheres of life.

So, six years ago, discovering that a nearby factory wanted thousands of rubber washers for petrol cans, Li and her friends discussed what they could do. They scraped together 18 yuan (about £3) and bought some old inner tyre tubes. With scissors they snipped and snipped away until their first order was completed.

Gradually, they earned enough money to buy a simple press to stamp out various other associated products—but it was three months before they earned any money.

Once, the press broke, and tears rolled down their cheeks. Then Li said: "Will tears do more than relieve our sorrow? No. Let's ask our customers at the factory if they will lend us the money for the repairs."

The workshop now has proper premises and equipment and produces thousands of pounds worth of rubber soles, heels and washers a year.

Men and women there earn equal wages—and all the workers, through an elected committee, decide how much money shall be spent on wages, how much on improvements and new equipment.

During the 1961 Spring Festival

ancipation—and happiness—seem natural to this young wife.
y ten years ago her lot would have been very different.

Dancers from the Peking Ballet bring traditional poise and grace to their art in a modern world.

TIA

Learning to live as individuals, valued members of the community, instead of being without rights and counted merely as their husbands' chattels

ther like Britain's Easter Bank liday) they had to work to mplete a shipyard order. "But it s worth it," said Li. "We women now responsible people. No ger nobodies without rights."

n Li's kitchen I saw no gadgets labour-saving devices. Every-ng was simple. Her basic kit-en equipment consisted of a fe, a chopping board and some n cooking pots. Cooking in-dients she buys loose—packaging lmost unknown.

Li's house is not very grand. It es not yet have running water. t some of her friends are more tunate. Under the rebuilding emes, they are gradually mov-, into apartment blocks where re is water and electricity.

Li still sleeps on a traditional inese wooden bed, covered with lts to make it softer.

While Li is at work, her young Chen is looked after in a local rsery - school run by three men in the area. It was started the initiative of one of these men, and fills a vital need.

Many of China's young mothers rk—in offices, textile mills, steel tories, as train and tram drivers, hnicians . . . all helping in the gent task of bringing China up date in a few short years.

Because this nursery is self-porting, toys and bedding are brought from home, but the young girls on the staff are de-voted to the children. Their in-genuity in making things for them to play with compensates for the lack of equipment.

On Sunday, a great family day, everyone is reunited. Li and her family go to visit Li's mother who cooks special meals of pork and vegetables for them.

Once in a while, Li's husband, Wang-Shu, takes the whole family out to one of the many restaurants in the city, where a meal for four, of rice, meat and vegetables, costs as little as 1½ yuan (about 5s.).

Li's daughter, Sun, a student who, among other things, learns engineering at school, is lucky—she will be able to marry someone of her choice. Before 1949 all marriages were arranged.

But old customs can't be changed overnight, and this battle between China's old and new was mirrored in a Peking divorce court I visited.

Lung, 23, wanted to end his marriage to Tia, his 25-year-old wife. Three judges, two of them women, sat on a raised platform in the courtroom, which was more like a schoolroom.

Lung and Tia sat just in front of them. This was the second hear-ing; the lower court had ruled that the divorce should be granted,

but Tia was not really satisfied.

Without ceremony, the chief judge asked Lung to state his case. This he did frankly and without fear for 45 minutes. For him the marriage was over. He no longer loved his wife.

True, he had had no major dif-ferences with her on basic issues but in the 18 months of marriage he had come to the conclusion that he had made a mistake.

He accused his wife of spending too much time at her factory and not enough with the family (by which he meant *his* family). He didn't like the way she dressed and didn't think she was attractive.

Things went wrong from the beginning, he continued. Tia's family had been annoyed because he did not keep up the old custom of sending a member of his family to fetch her to the wedding. Lung said that even this early in the marriage Tia accused him of not treating her properly.

When he wanted to discuss prob-lems with her, she said he only wanted his wishes obeyed. He even went to her mother to try to sort things out, but got no help.

Finally, his wife had threatened to blacken his name if he gained a divorce, so that no other girl would want him.

Then it was Tia's turn. She spoke for nearly as long as Lung. She was adamant that she did not want the divorce.

The families had taken a big part in bringing about the marriage and in the beginning she was not as sure about Lung as she might have been. But they had a great deal in common and could help each other.

His education was better than

hers and he ought to have helped her. Instead, he criticised her for taking too big a part in life out-side the home.

As for not liking her clothes and saying she was unattractive, this was the first she had heard about it.

Time and time again she told the judges that she thought her marriage could be successful if only her husband would relent.

The judges were clearly puzzled. Obviously, Lung would not change his mind.

Then they asked him to leave the court for a few minutes. They urged Tia to agree to a divorce. They pointed out that she could expect nothing but unhappiness tied to a man who no longer loved her. But she stood firm.

By sympathetic questioning the judges gradually discovered that Tia thought a divorce would be a disgrace. She felt that her family would blame her for failure and that her friends might shun her.

The judges explained that the law gave every married couple the right to end the marriage without blame to either side if reconcilia-tion failed. No one was disgraced by divorce.

Two days later the court gave judgment that the divorce should be granted. Tia's friends were asked to give her special help during such a trying time . . .

The unfinished story of Tia is the story of the struggle of 350 million Chinese women to adjust themselves to a new and challeng-ing situation.

For their nation is making tre-mendous changes in a very short time . . . changes which took Britain centuries to complete.

155

It was cold and wet, and she only had one blanket but next morning she was taken to a safe house where she stayed for ten days. Then friends came to fetch her with the news that a telegram had been received from London to say that the Republic of South Africa could not reclaim her and that she would be given asylum in Basutoland. Reassured of safety she drove off with friends to Maseru where she stayed with a comrade for three months until the house at Mafateng where we met her was found.

When we met her she was looking after nine small children. The house was in a bad state of repair and water came in through the roof when it rained. Despite the lack of furniture and the primitive cooking arrangements it was well kept, and she had done what she could to make it a home.

She lived on a very low income. All her money came from either the Human Rights Welfare Committee, which gave her two pounds a month, or from private individuals who helped her, some of whom were from abroad. Her main problem was the fact that she could not get any work. In the small town of Mafeteng where she lived there was very little work which was suitable but as 'marked' as she was it was unlikely that anyone would employ her. For a women used to the rough and tumble of trade union organising, despite the occupation that childcare offered, the loneliness and isolation was very hard for her to bear. Her banishment was set to last as long as the Government chose, and as was often remarked at the time, unlike a prison sentence that starts and ends, with this punishment there was no end at all.

She was still a fighting woman when I saw her and she had lost none of her fire. She told me how she had thrown a couple of reporters who intruded on her privacy out of the house, saying, 'Why is the Fatherland interested in me? Your paper and the special branch know all there is to know about me. You are just a couple of narks working for a government which is worried because I am still alive.'

My trip to South Africa took place over thirty years ago. Sadly many of the people I talked to and stayed with are now dead, but the situation has changed radically. Nelson Mandela was on the run when I was there, Bram Fischer was the hard working advocate doing whatever he could in the anti-apartheid struggle, Molly Fischer was active, though under a banishment order from 1950 – which I still have in my possession – so could not attend any meetings, Helen Joseph was active although already subject to various bans before her house arrest, and Violet and Eli Weinberg, with their daughter Sheila, were stalwarts of the movement. Except for Nelson and Sheila, all are now dead. And South Africa is to have a one-man-one-vote election, and Nelson Mandela might well be the first black president of the Republic of South Africa.

I had barely recovered from the trip to South Africa when, in 1963, the Chinese, for whom I was working at time, invited me to spend a month or so in China as the guest of the government. My employment in the Hsinhua News Agency in London had given me the opportunity to appreciate the Chinese methods of work so I welcomed the invitation and made arrangements for my two children, then 18 and 16, to be looked after by my brother and his wife.

I travelled to China via Moscow on my own as my husband Roland, who made at least two trips a year to China as a trade consultant, was already there. It was the loneliest journey I ever made. Most of my fellow travellers were Russian and since I was the only one with a ticket all the way to Peking, I was not exactly flavour of the month. From Moscow I caught a Chinese plane, and things were more friendly. Flying to China is hazardous food wise. Whenever we stopped it seemed to be a meal time and I think I must have had five dinners that day. The old lags knew the score and ate very little at each stop. We novices suffered by trying to please our hosts by eating everything we were offered.

When I arrived in Peking Airport I was greeted by a 'welcoming party' who met me and told by a uniformed official that my luggage would not be examined as I was the guest of the government and I was free to leave the airport whenever I wished. 'I hope you enjoy your stay in our country,' he said. I was most impressed. I soon discovered that this sort of action was typical of the way the Chinese behaved. The man who made the decision not to examine your luggage came to tell you so himself. If you asked a question in a factory, for example, the person taking you around was not the person who answered – it was the person actually doing the work you were asking about. Everywhere I went this seemed to happen and at the same time things are done in a calm orderly way with no pushing and shoving. One-up-man-ship seemed to be absent.

I was given an interpreter, and a busy tour of the country, but I chose the places I would visit at each place I was in. I was not refused any venues although it is true I was not so stupid as to ask to see sensitive venues like arms factories or military establishments. I wanted to get a picture of working life, and everyday life, particularly for women in China.

For most people, the day started early: at around 5.30am everything was moving. Although food was rationed either by ticket or price there appeared to be enough to feed everyone at a nutritionally adequate level if not at a 'balanced' diet level. Cotton was rationed, but wool and silk, shoes, and carpets used by rural families as bedcovers were not.

I visited a busy department store, and the longest queue was for bicycles. The design of products was good, and some of the textile designs

CHILDREN'S RIGHTS

Alternative Education

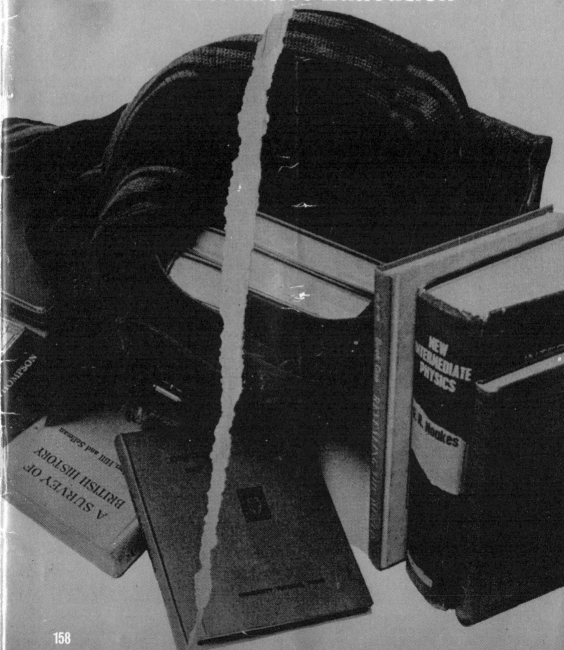

were like ones you might find in Habitat. The design of furniture was very good although I did notice that there was much 'kitsch' on sale as well.

One visit was to the Peking municipal jail where I was told there were 1,000 inmates, with 100 of them women. All of them had been through the courts, with forty per cent of the prisoners convicted as counter-revolutionaries and sixty percent as criminals. The aim of the system was to reform prisoners through education and work, and all of the prisoners worked except for those who rejected the basis of the prison regime and its ideas. The prison considered it a punishment to be denied work and forced by circumstances to be idle. None of the cells had locks on the doors, and the security of the prison was maintained by an electrified fence. Newspapers and magazines are provided with the *People's Daily* distributed every day, one to each group of five prisoners. The pattern of the day was a nine-hour day shift or an eight-hour night shift. The rest of the time was allocated as follows: eight hours for sleeping, one hour for cultural activity, and two hours for study. The remainder of the time was taken up by meals, bathing – cold once a day in summer and hot once a week in winter – laundering clothes, cell cleaning and other domestic chores. There was one rest day per week. Once a month, groups of prisoners are taken on a trip to either a historic building, an exhibition, or a factory. There was a hospital, with an acupuncture unit, attached to the jail, and regular medical checks were carried out. The hospital could cope with ordinary diseases, but those who had serious complicated medical conditions were transferred to other hospitals. Sometimes relatives are called to collect the patient and take them to a suitable hospital.

There was a parole system in operation and also a system of awards for good work and good behaviour. A prisoner who had completed a sentence and satisfied the jail authorities that he/she was reformed could apply for work in the prison as a freeman where proper wages were paid.

The Central Institute of Drama was a major educational establishment, situated in Peking since 1949, having moved from Yenan after the liberation. There I was met by a representative of the president's office and the director of the Marxist Leninist Research Group. I also met one of the presidents, Lip Po Chou, who had been on the Long March.

Many people apply for admission to the Institute but only a small proportion are admitted. The year I was there 700 applied and 20 were admitted. There were four courses in the Institute, divided with strict allocation of time, with political education taking up twelve per cent of teaching time, artistic theory and history of drama ten per cent, the specialised courses sixty per cent, and culture and literature, foreign languages, musical appreciation, and appreciation of literature eighteen per cent. The courses were for three years with additional course for directors for four years. The Institute has the status of a university but could select its students before the universities.

When I was there students numbered 430 with 124 teachers and lecturers. Administrative staff numbered 160 and the library held approximately 170,000 books. Every student had to spend one month a year in productive labour in the countryside working with the peasants and workers. During this month they would also help the military, living as the soldiers lived. Through work of this kind the students got used to the combination of hard manual and rural labour and military life, developing a level of respect for the views of both peasants and workers. It helped them overcome the feeling that manual work was degrading.

When the students qualified they were found jobs by the Institute. Some were sent to drama groups in the factories, some to the Peoples Liberation Army, and some to city and provincial theatre companies. Students were much welcomed in the communes because of the great help they could give in organising song and dance groups which are so much appreciated by rural communes in China.

Thirty per cent of the students were women. The leadership of the school said that whilst this may be unsatisfactory it was due to the small number of parts written for women. The leadership was somewhat embarrassed when I pressed them on this question. I asked why did they not persuade playwrights to put more women into their work. They replied that the plays they wanted to see written were those which reflected real life and men were still more active than women. They hoped this situation would change.

As I was particularly interested in the work of women I visited Beijing Embroidery Co-operative, which had 3,000 members. Formed in 1949 by the Federation of Women in Beijing it was first a co-operative factory and later also a training organisation with 200 courses in embroidery. Once a woman had completed a course she could then join the co-operative and receive work from it. Work was either done in small factories, at home, or in small groups. The establishment I saw was the central depot where the work was prepared, the cottons selected, patterns created, and the packages dispatched to working members wherever they were working. There were 700 basic designs and 50 separate items produced, some using simple cross stitch and others more elaborate stitches and designs. Many wall pictures are produced. The finished items were collected by one of the four branch offices in Beijing and packed off to the shops or sent abroad.

Visits to kindergartens, lunch at the summer palace, a visit to the Revolutionary Museum, visits to four schools, to the head offices of the women's associations, to canteens, to the house of a heroine of labour – whose award was not for outstanding work in a factory but for pulling her family up from a drunken, unemployable unit to a self-motivating group – to a dinner with the female Vice-Minister of Construction, to nearly all the major sights in and around Beijing, though not the Great Wall, rounded off my stay in Beijing. On my final eveing I attended a banquet held in the Great Hall of the People where there were 5,000 guests. The next day we left by air for Wuhan.

My first task in there was to take a rest. The Chinese are very keen on their guests taking rests. First of all they consider it is good for the guests and secondly it gives them time to assess how trips are going and decide if any changes should be made.

Like the students at the Institue in Beijing I was also taken on a number of visits to rural communes. The day started with breakfast of a lightly boiled egg mixed with rice and a cup of tea followed by a full meal as soon as everybody was dressed. This routine was based on the needs of the commune workers who required a good meal to start the day as they would not eat again until they returned home in the late afternoon. My day consisted of listening to long speeches by the commune leadership which were interesting but tended to be boring when strings of figures were read out. But I was grateful that they took so much trouble to tell me about their work.

In Canton the visits I paid were rather low key compared with the rest of the trip, a sort of pleasure run before I had to go back to England. There were two visits to the opera, the Park of Culture, the Canton Fair where there were a great many English firms taking part, and a farewell dinner at the Snake restaurant.

My visit to China was the first eastern country I had visited. I am in fact a poor traveller. I am generally nervous and stressed. In China I was neither. Everyone was calm and respected one's needs. I made great friends with my interpreter and in 1992 when he was stationed in Britain I made contact with him again. I was sorry to see him return to China.

Of all the countries I have visited I liked the ideology and practice of China best. I could see more hope in their regime than in others. It was therefore a terrible shock and disappointment when in 1989 the authorities chose to mow down the students and workers demonstrating in Beijing's Tiananmen Square. Nothing could excuse such attacks and in the course of time the Chinese themselves realised the enormity of their crime. Such an occurrence does not invalidate China's positive points – it means that if this price were to recur one would refuse to pay it.

Human Rights

XI
A Second Home

Resources in Education

The School Meals Service

From its Beginnings to the Present Day

EDUCATION ACT
School Meals Service

MENU
Roast beef and vegetables

Apple pie and custard

NAN BERGER

I VERY MUCH ENJOYED the experiences in those various countries, mainly non-European, I visited. To see different cultures, different ways of living, had been exciting and stimulating but I never felt I would like to live in any of them. I had often yearned to spend more time in France, especially in a house in the countryside which I owned myself. I had spent many holidays – indeed practically every holiday – in France since I was a teenager and the family, Roland, Carol and Vicki, had spurned holidays in Britain because we had been always unlucky with the weather. I loved France – and still do – not so much for the cities but for the rural life and its attitude to food. So, in the late sixties when I was earning fairly decent money editing a magazine devoted to hotel and catering management, I decided to start looking for a house in south west France 'in need of refurbishment', in a place where a relative also had a house. I put it to myself that this was an investment which would produce a pension in my old age. Which it did but that is another story.

By this point in time I had written a few books which brought in some cash, and I earned a middle-sized living as a freelance journalist as well as being a partner in a typesetting business. I counted my money, and the figures looked possible. I decided to take a chance and started my search.

I did not have to look long. The house I had conjured up in my sleeping moments quickly came into daytime reality. My sister and I had planned a few days in Dieppe. Just before we left my relative offered us her house on the borders of the Charente and the Dordogne for up to a month if we needed it. It was November and the first night there was very cold – but we learned to cope with oil stoves and log fires and started to look for my fantasy house. By some sort of miracle it came into view at the end of a lane. It was extraordinarily like my dream house, or so I persuaded myself. The attached barn was twice the size of the house, the surrounding patch of land grew fruit trees – plums, apples, cherries, and a grape vine – all in need of care and attention. It had a well with a rather pretty well-head and a *citerneau* though well past its best and probably quite useless. Inside, the house had a large room with an immense fireplace, a large kitchen with nothing in it, and upstairs, in the granary, it was one big space, enough to make three rooms.

However, finding the owner was not so easy. I had taken a decision not to deal with agents so somehow I had to find the owner myself. There was no one around to ask so we sat down on a stone wall to ponder. No one appeared, and there were no responses to the knocks we made on the few doors within walking distance. Sadly, we moved off to seek some lunch almost putting the house out of mind. But I could not leave it alone. Nothing would do but this very house. So back we went and found there was a small man on the lane feeding the tits which were sitting on his cap and shoulders. We put our question and I could hardly believe my ears when he said his sister owned the house and gave us he gave us her address in Vaux-Lavalette.

His sister was unfortunately adamant 'No,' she could not sell because of the *remembrement*. She tried to explain what the *remembrement* was and we all got bogged down in unmanageable technicalities.

Disheartened, we journeyed back to the house, to speak again to her brother, Marc Marcellot. He rushed back into his own house and emerged after a time with a book about France. 'It is published in England,' he said, 'so you will understand it,' and that his sister was talking rubbish. He read it like the 'instituteur exemplaire' that he was.

'One of the land problems of France has been the parcelisation of the soil,' he said, 'and the French Government have been trying to solve this since 1940. Fly over many parts of France and you will see a crazy quilt of thin strips; quite a modest farmer may often have ten or twenty different little fields, not next to each other but scattered over miles. This is partly a result of the equal inheritance laws, as farms were split up between sons and then the parcels changed hands. And it often makes modern mechanised farming extremely difficult. The policy of *remembrement* – literally, the piecing together of limbs – was initiated by Vichy and has continued ever since.'

After the policy had been carefully explained, we went back to Madame to tell her that according to her brother, there was not a problem. She explained that she had not realised that provided the buyer was aware of the proposals of *remembrement* the seller was protected and could sell in good faith. Together we sought out her husband who was working in the nearby forest and she explained that I wanted to buy the house and that I understood the proposals under the *remembrement* and would not oppose them.

I did not have to make an offer. The forester told me what he wanted, what he thought was a fair price. He said he did not want to bargain it was a 'take it or leave it' situation. I took it and we shook hands. The deal had been made and from that moment if either of us changed our mind we would forfeit ten per cent of the agreed price to the other party to the bargain. There was no change of mind on either side, and the sale preceded with the assistance of the local *notaire* and was settled in two months. When I finally looked into the proposals under the *remembrement* I found I had lost a rectangular strip at the west side of my two hectare plot but gained a strip slightly smaller on the east side which had the added the bonus of a mature cherry tree which flowered and fruited in great abundance each year.

In January 1973, I took my younger daughter Vicki and her partner, both of them architects, to the house with the intention of getting them working on plans to put the place in a state that allowed me to live in it, albeit a bit roughly. They took one look at the place and strode off for a walk. Through broken floor boards I could see about two feet of water in the cellar, and there was glass in only three of the seven windows, the front door was swinging on one hinge and the external big barn was full of machinery. The roof had holes in it, and broken tiles were lying on the ground. When the two architects returned from the walk looking even more fed up they took another slow look around the house, packed up their drawing board and paper and pencils, turned to me and said 'You might have told us you had bought a wreck' and marched off to the car.

When we got to the hotel it was already dark but there was just time for a soothing bath and a change of clothes.

At dinner we hardly spoke until I noticed that after a few glasses of house red both of them were taking out their pens and making marks on the paper table cloth. By the end of the meal they had sorted out what needed to be done to make the house habitable and announced that they were ready to talk to the builder the following morning. They explained what they were proposing even included some work which was longer term like re-flooring the granary and mending the roof of the barn. It seemed an admirable start to me. When we met the builder the next morning the first thing I did – having previously asked him if he would, with his mate, do the job – was pass a fairly large amount in notes to him using the car bonnet as a desk, and Marcel Reynard, acting for himself and Andre Gillot, gave me a receipt. Later when we had been round the house and discussed each item Marcel said, 'It will be ready by Pâques,' and apart from the staircase it was. The opinion of the builders was that cutting a beam for a new staircase might mean serious movement in the building, and they suggested that if we wanted this to be done Jon, Vicki's partner, should cut it himself. He did not but wisely bowed to hands-on experience. For the time it took to plan the relocation of the staircase and get it made we used a ladder.

When I returned at Easter I opened the front door, which was now a rather interesting shade of grey, and was amazed and delighted to see the dazzling white pine floor, the new door at the far end of the room and the newly mended windows and shutters. There was a new floor in the kitchen also and a homemade ladder to reach the floor above where there were bedrooms with their own rooflights. It all looked incredibly beautiful to me and I could not wait to start living there. In fact, I had to wait one more day because we realised too late for the shops that we had no beds to sleep on although the car was loaded to the roof with bedding and blankets.

After an early breakfast at the hotel in St Seveirin where my sister and I stayed we shot off to the large furniture shop just outside the village on the road to Riberac, Meubles David, and looked at beds. We bought two single beds for 542 francs, about fifty pounds at the exchange rate at the time, complete with foam mattresses, all covered in striped ticking. The shop agreed to deliver that day. We also bought a gas cooker. We borrowed some chairs, made a table from an old salt box which we found in the garden, put an even older door on top of the salt box and we were in the business of serving meals! The salt box was like a small coffin on short legs used to salt meat in order to preserve it. We used it for many months but sadly it fell apart eventually as when the salted wet wood dried out the dowelling fell out and the wood cracked into strips.

We had no light for a few days but then Marc Marcelot and the farmer across the lane, Monsieur Lefaye, came and fixed up a wire from Marc's house and we had light for free. Marc would take no cash. Later when I wanted to buy a fridge I told Marc that I must pay for the electricity. He said 'no way', so I said 'no fridge'. In two days time the man who sold fridges in Riberac was on the doorstep saying he would deliver me a fridge because Marc had paid for one! So, I chose a fridge and gave Marc his money back.

When our well water on which we relied was analysed it was deemed unfit for human consumption. Another farmer gave us permission to draw water from his outside tap and even brought a bucket or two for us when he was passing. It wasn't until the next winter that the mains water came and I fitted a bath, a washbasin and a flushing lavatory. A very skilled local carpenter made a working counter in the kitchen and I bought a stainless-steel sink of splendid proportions. A table was made by a local joiner, some chairs brought from my London house where they were surplus to requirements, along with a few rugs and two more beds and we were beginning to feel well equipped.

La Bouteillerie – the name of the hamlet where the house was situated – was a joy to everyone who visited. Our neighbours were two farmers, one with five young children, another with one grown up son working for the government plant in Périgueux which printed bank notes, and a valued school master. The children of Roger and Paulette Priat brought in our daily ration of unpasteurised milk. All five of them came at the same time and shook hands all round. In ten minutes they left to go home and shook hands all round again. We never missed this ritual, and I always considered the ability to touch a great aid to friendship and equality. My other neighbours were Monsieur Lepinski, a Pole, and his wife, and Marc Marcelot, whom we'd first met finding the house. He was a retired school teacher, charming but lazy. He had his meals with a family nearby and almost always slept there. In the morning when he came down our lane he had with him a pocketful of walnuts which he cracked on the ground and would immediately be surrounded by dozens of birds who had been waiting in the bushes. One day when a friend and I were taking a nap under the fig tree I woke to see a pair of feet in French carpet slippers. Funny, I thought, I didn't know Miriam had bought a pair of French bedroom slippers. She hadn't. It was Marc who had lain down between us and was already asleep!

Across the other side of the lane lived Monsieur et Madame Lefayes, and Alain their grown-up-son. Alain was rather a mysterious young man who lived, so they said, quite a riotous nightlife in the nearby town. His farming instincts overrode all others. One day in February I saw a flock of wild geese flying over his house. They flew in a spear shaped flock and the sound of the wings beating was very pleasant. It was altogether a beautiful sight and I told Alain about it. 'But you can't eat them,' he said. 'If you want a goose you can get one from our flock!' I tried to convince him that it was the beauty of them I liked but he just replied, 'Yes, but you can't eat them.'

All these neighbours helped me a great deal and often popped in for a drink. I think they liked our family and friends because they didn't behave like rich townies. We didn't laze around in bikinis while they were sweating it away in the fields, nor did we ask them to clean our home or till our garden, or regale them with stories of how much more civilised life in London was. We didn't use the builders in the nearby town who had set themselves up to renovate houses for the English, we gave work to our neighbours, lent them our tools. In return they cut our field for hay, put their tractor in our barn, and were on hand when anything went wrong.

For seven years we enjoyed the beauty of the landscape, the garden, and the house itself. Most of the people who came to stay made some work contribution as I charged only just enough rent to cover the outgoings.

It was not everyone's cup of tea. It really was the simple life and some of them who said they liked the simple life didn't like it at all when they realised it meant cold water for washing now and again and draughts on gusty days plus wasps and flies to cope with in the summer. Gradually things changed as we got piped water, a bathroom and lavatory and proper water heating equipment, but once these things are in a sort of erosion starts. You start to 'need' other things like wall-to-wall carpets, matching curtains, plastered walls instead of rough stone ones, easy chairs instead of the uprights we had sat on around the table after supper, a neat garden, better wine, fewer draughts and eventually central heating loomed. I never got to the point of putting this in although I could see it coming.

During a few of those years I made a good friend of Marc Marcelot whose wit and jollity made a visit from him something very special. We did crosswords together in English and French. His English was about as good as my French and he was very fond of little odd practical witticisms. He also taught me some phrases one would not normally find in a French dictionary. I was greatly saddened that he died when I was not in France but my daughter Carol represented me at his funeral and reported that the procession following his coffin to the church was at least a quarter of a mile long. I respected him and loved him dearly, learning much from him, but I did not realise what a splendid character he really was. The obituary in a Périgueux newspapers by A. Devesne, Inspecteur d'academie honaire (Universite de Périgueux), showed the man in glowing terms and gave information which Marc modestly never revealed in his communication with me.

On the 20 May, the funeral of Monsieur Mercelot took place at Bouteille-Saint-Sebastien (Dordogne), attended by an impressive gathering of friends and admirers. M. Marcelot was a retired teacher, who for almost his entire career taught in the neighbouring small village of Lusignac.

His activities as a pedagogue were so remarkable as to be legendary.

In a mixed school, burdened with a class of forty four (thirty six of school age and eight older students), his teaching was of such quality that not only did one hundred per cent of his students pass their certificate of studies exam, but achieved the same success in their *baccalaureate.*

He also created a school co-operative, countryside activities, started sports teams and of course a collection of books about the Dordogne. He solved (well before it was the fashion) the two problems of equality of opportunity and permanent education.

Of an astounding erudition, for two years running, he won the prize of 100,000 old francs. The third year he was asked not to compete in order to give the other competitors a chance. He presented these 200,000 francs to the co-operative.

As a prisoner of war he escaped and arrived in Lusignac to learn that his brother had been tracked down by the Gestapo. He just had time to embrace his mother and left to join the Maquis.

A master who from every point of view honours the University.

Instead of central heating came a large increase in my work as a journalist along with the realisation that getting to la Bouteillerie five times a year as I had been doing, was virtually impossible. I was getting a bit fed up of preparing the place for casual 'tenants' who did not always 'leave as found' although some of my friends and family frequently left it in better shape than they found it, and I was facing a situation where I had to either spend real money on the place or sell it since the money invested in it represented my pension.

So with cries of shame from some of my friends, I steeled myself to put it on the market and then sold it in a matter of weeks. It was a big wrench and one of the things I miss most. I took very fond memories of the place with me, such as the time when my very good friend Harry Baines stayed there to paint. He produced many paintings of the wonderful roses which Marc Marcelot grew around his gate and of the house and surrounding country, enough to mount a major exhibition in London at the Rotunda Gallery in 1978. Harry's wife Pauline, herself a book designer, was his partner in his painting work. She managed his exhibitions, work schedule and often set him up outside when he was not too keen to paint. She had a major influence on him which was all to the good. She too was a la Bouteillerie fan and made many improvements to the running of the house. I compensated this loss by buying a not so rural small house called Church Rise on the edge of the village of Walsham le Willows in Suffolk, where my friends and family met together at weekends and sometimes for a week in the summer.

One rather exciting thing I did at Walsham was to organise with some colleagues, notably Harry and Pauline Baines, a show of painting and drawings in Priory Room, the local village hall, which happened to be right opposite my house.

We invited five artists to exhibit their work under the title *Suffolk Meeting Point – an exhibition of paintings and drawings by artists with Suffolk connections*. We set up a committee of five participating artists with Pauline Baines as chairman, myself as 'manager' and Margaret Pryor as press officer.

Borrowing screens from a school in nearby Stowmarket, lighting from my nephew Nico Stubbs, and using bits and pieces of furniture such as tables and chairs from my house helped to keep costs down. As a committee we reckoned £50 from each of the participating artists ought to cover all costs including advertising, the hire of the hall for three days, transport for screens, and wine for the private view on the Friday before the exhibition was open to the public. There was to be no admission fee nor was there to be any commission taken on sales of the pictures.

By the time the hanging was completed it all looked very elegant and professional. Each artist had two large screens set at right angles making a sort of open cubicle. Lots were drawn to decide the position of screens for each artist and all were lit from overhead spots. The walls of the Priory Room were not suitable for direct hanging. The private view on the evening before the show opened was a 'full house' half an hour before we opened the doors. A glass of wine was served and the buying began. We were staggered at the interest.

It was 10pm before the last guest departed and the last glass washed up. Then all the artists and helpers moved over to Church Rise for their party – a hot meal and plenty of drinks. We faced the next day with our confidence buoyed up by the enthusiasm at the private view. We had started our advertising campaign around the beginning of August with a beautifully designed poster by Sheila for use in shops, on trees and gateposts, in parks, and in the windows of friendly householders, and had written articles for the *Bury Free Press, East Anglian Times, Radio Orwell, Walsham Observer* and invited representatives of their papers to attend the exhibition. They did, and they took pictures which were printed the following day.

I submitted a report to the committee which detailed an attendance of 350 people, sales of £1,713, and costs of £240, which worked out at £48 per artist. I said, 'it was a great success and worth the effort,' and despite some necessary improvements to the organisation, particularly the sales documentation, from the village point of view it was worth doing.

The extension of my paid work for my major client continued at Walsham, but because of badly drawn up contracts attracted no more money. But it was an interesting assignment and as I was sixty-nine I dared not risk termination. Walsham was only 90 miles from London, almost commuting distance, so I could cope with the work much more easily than I could from south west France, and the journeys to and fro were much cheaper and of course less time consuming.

Real 'retirement' came when I was 70 and lost my main journalist job, the editorship of a magazine for managers in the hotel and catering industry. Now I really needed my pension so there was no alternative to selling Church Rise and 'buying' a pension, too late of course to provide more than a basic income but I had no mortgage and two generous daughters and the ability to earn a few bob from time to time.

Leaving Church Rise was not such a wrench as leaving la Bouteillerie. The village was dominated by 'landed gentry' families and was a typical class-structured English village. I made friends with the small farmers, the shop keepers, the local garage, and I was near enough to my sister who lived twelve miles away to ensure that I was not isolated. It amused me to see how the class structure worked. The shopkeepers used a different voice when they served the 'gentry' and some of them became quite subservient. The gentry did actually talk to me on occasions and even invited me to their houses for drinks (but not for dinner) but I could feel that I was not quite accepted. They invited you into the fringe of their camp only so you wouldn't join the opposition but their acceptance was superficial.

I had taken the editorship of the hotel and catering magazine, a forerunner of *Hospitality,* official magazine of the Hotel and Catering and Institutional Management Association (HCIMA), when it was a small in-house magazine and moved it through many stages until it was an A4 size monthly journal carrying some £18,000 per month of advertising, many full colour, with a print run of 22,000. The bulk of readers were managers in hotels, contract catering and welfare catering.

One of the reasons why *Hospitality* attracted so much advertising from firms processing and marketing food and from those making catering equipment was that a large majority of School Meals Organisers (SMOs) in Britain were members of the HCIMA. SMOs were managers of the services which, in the seventies and early eighties when the school meals service was at its peak, controlled an annual budget for food alone in excess of £183,000,000. As such any magazine which could reach them could rely on getting a fair proportion of food and equipment advertising.

The SMOs were in a special position in the HCIMA. They were a separate section with their own constitution and officers and managed their own affairs under the umbrella of HCIMA. The reason SMOs were in the HCIMA arose from the fact that when the school meals service expanded, the result of the clause in the 1944 Education Act which stipulated that a meal should be provided for every child who desired one, the only people trained for such a job were members of the Institutional Managerial Association – a forerunner of the HCIMA. Highly trained in welfare catering they were the only body capable of managing the production of such large numbers of meals and of maintaining quality of food and hygiene conditions. The local education authorities who employed the SMOs specified in their recruitment literature that the IMA, later the HCIMA, qualification was obligatory for those seeking the post of SMO.

At the peak of the School Meals Service 5.7 million meals a day were produced supplying over seventy per cent of the children in school with meals. The price to the parent was 12p per day which was 62.7 per cent of the actual cost of the meal, 19.5p.

The more I learned about the school meals service, the more I leant over backwards to help them all I could. I helped them with their publicity and very early on in my time with the HCIMA I took on the responsibility for producing the *National Association of School Meals Organisers (NASMO) Handbook.*

Out of the blue the HCIMA decided that it could no longer afford to give NASMO the financial support it had provided since it was founded in 1966. This financial support was considerable, covering secretarial support, provision of rooms for meetings, auditing of accounts, taking postal and telephone enquiries and considerable other support, included providing many of the services which a trade union normally gives their members, advising on cases of wrongful grading, unfair dismissals, and underpayment. Ultimately NASMO decided to divorce itself from the HCIMA and so from the ashes of disaster arose the *Local Authority Caterers Association* (LACA), totally independent although many of the members retained their membership in the HCIMA. It recruited nearly all the members of the former NASMO, took over the NASMO handbook which I had edited for nearly a quarter of a century, and me with it.

The advertisement revenue made the sort of money that enabled LACA to undertake national campaigns and make a major contribution to the fight to prevent further cuts in the school meal service.

Thatcher's government had of course protected itself against the allegation that it wished to kill the service altogether by neatly passing the buck to local authorities. First it had abolished the direct subsidy on meals and by the Education 1980 (No. 2) Act had removed the statutory right of a meal for every child who wanted one, with only the mandatory free meals remaining for those who qualified. A local authority could continue supplying meals to those who wished for one but the cost had to be met by the local authority and compete with demands from other educational expenditures such as books, writing materials, and teachers' salaries. Moves toward the privatisation of the school meal service were made sharper by the introduction of compulsory competitive tendering.

Competitive tendering may well commend itself to those who believe that local authority services are inefficient and expensive, but their judgment may well be altered when they appreciate that competitive tendering is now compulsory. It has been suggested that compulsory competitive tendering is a means of finding out whether the school meals service can be run more cheaply and the subsidy lessened. It supporters say that competitive tendering would bring to public attention the detailed costings of school meals services, and, in forcing local education authorities to put in tenders to run their own services, create pressure to compare public and private enterprise in a whole range of services provided by the local authority – including catering, refuse collection and street cleaning, cleaning of buildings, ground maintenance, and vehicle maintenance.

The government got its power to impose compulsory competitive tendering from the Local Government Act 1988. Before the Act came into force local education authorities already had the *choice* of going to tender for local services and this system worked well. Under the new scheme of compulsory competitive tendering for the provision of school meals hundreds of tenders had to be sought. Each authority had to put out a number of invitations to tender because not many firms of contract caterers – if any at all – had the capability of tendering for the whole of the school meals programme, and most limited capability in even the smallest of areas.

In 1985 some authorities had tested the water. In Kent, a detailed specification for the Sevenoaks division of the county was prepared, stating a three-year contract period and a reasonable level of wages based on local circumstances. Of the twenty invitations issued six companies applied to view the service in operation but only one company finally submitted a bid. This was thoroughly investigated by the authority, and some surprising errors had to be corrected before the bid could be compared with the in-house costs. The comparison was judged to show that the private bid was in excess of in-house costs, and the service in Sevenoaks therefore remained with the authority's own catering organisation, however, the exercise created a mass of work for local officers and mounds of paperwork and costs. Since the service in Sevenoaks was already efficiently run and provided a meal of high nutritional quality the exercise in competitive catering contributed little to improving the service.

Essex was another county to make a trial of in-house efficiency. A primary school and a secondary school were chosen for individual contracts for one year. Tender documents were widely distributed but the response was disappointing. For both schools the costs of the lowest tenders were higher than the costs of the in-house service. Nevertheless the authority went ahead and awarded the one-year contract for the secondary school to a local firm. Even though the authority was providing them with free premises, and fuel and water, equipment maintenance and repairs were recharged back to the authority, and the contractor was only responsible only for cleaning of the kitchen and dining areas, the contractor was losing money and withdrew at the end of the year,

If contractors were successful in winning a large slice of tenders for the service it meant the end for the service as a whole. They could serve inferior meals and the authority would have great difficulty in making them improve. They could go into liquidation. They could sell their businesses to other managements which might well be less interested in providing nutritious meals for school children than they themselves were, and at any time they could withdraw their service. Any of these occasions would give any government cause to look again at the need for providing a school meals service at all, and a service which has been providing food for children for eighty years would disappear. On the other hand if the contractors had failed to win bids, then the government of the day would have been forced to accept that the school meals service was efficient, and they would have lost their back-door battle for privatisation.

The school meals service may very well survive the threat of privatisation through in-house bids being more acceptable than those put in by private contractors. If this does happen the service will no doubt be attacked again by the government on some other front, unless those who stand to gain from the service take steps to defend it. It must be rebuilt into a real welfare service such as was envisaged by the Education Act of 1944, getting back to the high quality meals served in the sixties and early seventies when seventy per cent of children in school were eating a school meal.

Parents, who for the most part have taken little interest in the service, will have to realise that they are the ultimate customers. They pay out the cash both directly in dinner money and as ratepayers and payers of income tax. School meals are the lifeline to healthy eating for children from poor homes. As poverty increases, the lifeline becomes more important, and at least one nutritionist has said that the need for nutritious school meals is as great now as it was in 1906 when free meals started. Parents of young children especially have a duty to enter into campaigns to preserve the service and improve it, campaigns which must be based locally on individual schools or groups of schools. It is also the duty of school governors to give as much attention to school meals as part of the school day as to any other subject on the school agenda.

Much of the success of the school meals service rests with the head teachers. If the head teachers have a positive attitude it will be reflected in the parents' and teachers' actions. If a head teacher says to a new parent, 'Will Ron or Sue be bringing sandwiches?' then the child will probably turn up with a lunch box. If, on the other hand, the head says, 'Sue, or Ron, will be staying for lunch with us, I hope?' it's probable that the children will eat school meals throughout their stay in primary school and well into their early secondary years. Likewise, where heads have made proposals for lunchtime supervision to include teachers who are given time off in lieu or reasonable payment, there was good co-operation.

Today food is on the political agenda. There has never been a time when there was more talk about it, and there have been enough reports relating health and disease to diet to convince all but the most obdurate government that a proper food policy is necessary for the well-being of the nation. Some notable contributions to this debate included:

The Black Report – so called because Sir Douglas Black, formerly chief scientist at the Department of Health and later president of the Royal College of Physicians, was chairman of the working group which produced *Inequalities in Health* – was presented to the Secretary of State in April 1980. It was not published properly as are other reports of the same nature, but was circulated in only 260 duplicated copies made available on a Bank Holiday weekend. Major organisations including the National Health Service did not receive copies. *The Black Report* recommended that a school meal should be available, free of charge, to any child who wanted one.

The National Advisory Committee on Nutrition Education (NACNE) published a report in 1983 giving specific goals for dietary change over the next fifteen years based on the fact that a number of diseases in the UK are linked to diet.

One-man campaigns for legal and social change have in the past been successful but they are few and far between and generally not on very important matters. Going it alone is really not much good as a form of protest and invariably has very unpleasant consequences for those who undertake it. If you are going to try and change things the more people you have with you – working on your side – the stronger you will feel and the more impact you are likely to make. This not only applies to the big issues in life but to the small ones as well. We need support and friendship in life when things are all right. We need it even more in times of trouble.

My mate Benny

Now I know a bloke called Benny,
Who lived in a furnished flat,
Ate his meals off an old card table
And slept with a sewer rat.

One day his landlord said to him,
Wife and kids an' all
'As from tomorrow, the bath, use of,
Will cease to be available.'

Now my mate Ben, he knows his law,
He nips off to County Hall.
'Don't my rent come down,' he says,
'If the bath has "ceased to be available".'

So they open a file on my mate Ben
Called: 'The Bath, Holloway Road'
And slipped a memo in a memo box
With 'details of the aforesaid abode'.

But Benny's landlord knows his law
and his order an'all –
Benny's car got daubed with paint
And his tyres cut with a saw.

For ten nights running an alsatian dog
Barked its bollocks off
And while his youngest had the 'flu
The power got cut off.

Now Benny knows his law
And who protects who.
Benny nipped off to the law shop
To see the boys in blue.

'Yes sir, no sir, three bags full sir
But we can't help your sort
Unless you can prove in a court of law it was
Physical assault.'

Now yer copper's a legal expert on
physical assault, of course.
That's why we call them the law
And they call themselves the force.

That's why, last year, for robbing shops,
forty thousand got done –
But for bashing tenants – a crime most rare
It was only fifty-one.

The landlord sits in his easy chair.
The street's the place for Benny,
While the boys in blue help the few
Milk the loot from the many.

Michael Rosen

Even direct action does not bring 'instant' results. Legal
and social change comes only when there is enough pressure
to make the people in power realize that unless they make
concessions conflicts will develop into uncontrollable revolt.
But there are a good many examples in history to show that
if there are enough determined people working together the
law and all its supporting institutions has to give way.

Following this, in 1984 the DHSS Committee on Medical Aspects of Food Policy (COMA), when looking at direct and cardiovascular disease, highlighted the need to reduce fat intake.

In 1987 the Coronary Prevention Group, in association with the Assistant Masters and Mistresses Association, produced *Diet or Disease – A Case for School Meals Guidelines.*

School meal organisers must cease simply to carry out food policies formulated by someone else. Their knowledge of nutrition and their experience in persuading children to eat unfamiliar foods and offer menus which conform to a given nutritional formula make them key personnel in the shaping of the school meals service of the next decade. Social attitudes towards women and their role in society have a great deal to do with the trivialisation of food policies. Food is seen as women's work, and women's work is not regarded as important so food takes a low profile in life.

This attitude may be changing in some respects but basically it remains a deterrent to a real change in our attitude to food. If the inter-relation between food and health were to be recognised it would alter our attitude to the providers of food, and to the manufacturers of food, those big firms which are permitted to influence food policies and make huge profits in the process. It would also alter our attitude to what we eat at home and how we eat. If we truly believed that food was basic to good health would we continue to eat as we do, knowing that diet-related diseases such as heart disease alone costs the health service £323 million? Would we continue to allow unhealthy food to be served in hospital wards? Local authorities, who provide a great deal of food eaten away from the home – meals on wheels, old age pensioner clubs, food in swimming baths, town halls, as well as school meals – must take the lead and announce their intention to put quality first and money second rather than quality last as happens today.

The integration of school meals into the mainstream educational system – such as the 1944 Act envisaged – would mean that a cornerstone of food policy has been re-laid. There is no better place than the school to teach the rudiments of healthy eating, and the fact that the service has been destroyed is a sad reflection of our refusal to come to terms with the matter.

In 1940 Herwald Ramsbotham MP, president of the Board of Education, wrote in a foreword to a pamphlet issued by the National Union of Teachers, 'A canteen meal which is well planned, well cooked and well served has much to contribute to the child's general education for it promotes good health, leads to the formulation of good habits and gives many forms of useful knowledge which will have much practical value in later life,' – as true now as it was then.

I was glad to be able to continue my work around the school meals service when I was made a founder member of LACA and invited to attend any executive council meetings I wished as a consultant on editorial matters. I attended many interesting meetings and conferences and continued to edit the Handbook until 1992 when I passed it over to Dorothy Gardner whom I had been coaching up for some months. Travelling long distances and working long hours had become impossible because of ill health and the deficiencies of old age, so I bowed out as gracefully as I could using my new leisure to write and to fulfil my commitments as a governor of a local primary school. I also did the preparation necessary for me to tackle the help I gave once a week to the eight year olds who were having difficulty with their reading.

When, in 1990 I was co-opted as a governor of the school I welcomed the opportunity. I already knew the school well and liked its style and I could not turn my back on the opportunity to help with the management of a school and of education, especially if as I had a grandson of primary school age.

Half-way through my first term of office things changed. Some Whitehall whizz-kid had thought up the idea that schools should be locally managed by governors and eventually this was worked into the educational legislation. Governors became the managers of the schools and the government created the ridiculous situation where a number of lay people – some elected by parents, and some nominated by the local authority, some elected by teachers and some co-opted by all the above groups – were in charge. None were paid, contracted or given allowances for fares or time off work. Anyone could resign or just not turn up to meetings. None needed any knowledge of educational law or practice nor any special knowledge of the subject they were dealing with. They could if they so wished, sit and say nothing at meeting after meeting, and no one would complain. Training was offered but it was of a very general nature and often rather amateur in concept.

On paper being a governor sounds like an important ploy in local democracy but in reality it is a tricky piece of window dressing conceived by a Tory government determined to remove power from local authorities in the guise of giving power to the people. The task was extremely complex – dealing with finance within an inadequate budget; recruitment of staff; matters of pastoral care; formulating policies on bullying, general behaviour, smoking on school premises; communications within the school and with the outside community; maintenance of the school building; as well as all the obvious matters such as complying with the compulsory curriculum – and the governors had to work through committees with very limited powers, with all major decisions impossible to take without the presence of either the chairman or deputy. Inevitably, the policy change was to redirect power from local government not to the people but to the head teacher and a small group of governors acting in a clique, leaving the rest – those who know little of what is going on – to vote on other people's proposals. Those governors who sit it out in this sort of all powerful group and work really hard in order to keep their school on a reasonable keel on impossibly low budgets are to be commended for their hard toil although they might do better by opposing the government in its crack-pot schemes rather than doing the government's dirty work for it. One cannot help but feel sorry for those governors who have agreed to give their services only to find that they have neither the time nor the ability to play a positive role and are just voting fodder.

I wonder sometimes when one becomes adult. Indeed, I wonder what adult means. Does it start when you leave school? I doubt it. In my case it did not start when I left university because I never got there in the first place. For me, I think it started when my mother died and I realised that I faced whatever I had to face – or enjoy – without that solid personality behind me. It does not really matter whether one's mother really is a strong character: what matters is that she is your mother and more likely to stand by you, rightly or wrongly, than anyone else you are likely to meet. The other jump to adulthood was when I joined the Communist Party. Joining not only meant an introduction into another world with different people and new ideas, it was also like entering a new kind of college which compensated for not going to a traditional one. The discipline was strict, the rewards not obvious but there was almost immediate satisfaction in the education offered. It enabled one to relate events to each other. If the word 'fast' used as an adjective had been in vogue in those heady days, the words 'fast college' might have been used. The aim was to learn and everything else was subjugated to knowledge. So, what was so special about the education you got through the Communist Party? Partly it was because you learned as much from your comrades as you did from the tutors. You had opportunities to meet, on equal ground, people you would not meet in your normal environment. You not only learned facts, where to find them and how to interpret them. You learned to communicate with people from all walks of life and you learned how they thought. You learned what was going on in the world and how to understand it. How else could I have coped with the horrors of unemployment, the Holocaust, the collapse of the Soviet Union, the Yugoslavian disaster, the Gulf War, or even the actions of the Tory government in the last fifteen years?

When the Second World War ended we entered a world which promised to be different. The 1945 election gave the Labour Party a huge majority. The *Manchester Guardian* for 27 July 1945 proclaimed Britain's 'revulsion against Tory rule' and continued 'the country's overwhelming demonstration of desire to share in a New Order'. If Clement Attlee was not quite what the nation needed or desired he was at least recognisable as an honest representative of a progressive labour policy. The *Manchester Guardian* on its main page reported from Berlin that the majority of soldiers were thoroughly pleased by the results. 'Few indeed,' the special correspondent in Berlin reported, 'with personal experiences of the army in this war would question that the army as a whole thinks predominantly in terms of the political left – much of this is not so much clear-cut thinking on Party lines as rather a general desire for improved social conditions, greater economic security, and a foreign policy which will not be allowed to drift another generation into war. Education for his children is a subject that the solider who is a married man thinks about a great deal and the desire of a much wider chance of education is another factor in the army's progressive political thinking.'

The punitive rule and attack on children and food by the Tories can be dated from Margaret Thatcher's Act when she was Minister of Education that cut milk in schools. It was one of her most damaging early contributions attacking the welfare state, outlined as an agenda, ten years earlier, in her maiden speech as a new MP when she had attacked local government. It was the beginning of a twenty-five-year fight to 'kill' local government, to the point where it was merely adjunct to central government. I cannot recall one piece of legislation by the Tories during the lengthy term of office during the nineteen eighties which helped people out of the poverty trap. Nor for that matter any legislation which benefitted the poor rather than the rich.

By the year 1994 the country – including people who normally voted Conservative had become totally disenchanted with Tory government with its wrongdoing and incompetence. In this atmosphere of despair and lack of all hope for change, unemployment remained high, job satisfaction decreased daily until one day in April we woke up to the realisation that the situation in South Africa was about to produce an election result that galvanised the world into a much more hopeful frame of mind.

We had watched the negotiations between Nelson Mandela and President de Klerk move from bitter conflict to uneasy co-operation and then into full co-operation between two men who had been enemies – the kind of enmity which had taken place against a violent background of mass killing.

As time moved along it became a little bit more obvious each day that the ANC was going to carry the people with them and win the election. The eyes of the world were on one of the century's hot spots. One of the most spectacular elections involving around nineteen million people who had never voted before. Everyone held their breath as election day grew nearer. When would the bloodbath start? We watched daily but it never came. The good sense of Nelson Mandela and President de Klerk never allowed the skirmishes which occurred to develop into major incidents. The infrastructure necessary to carry out an election was put in place in a matter of weeks. There were mistakes and delays which elsewhere would have ruined such an election, but in South Africa the people waited for hours for lost ballot papers to be found or reprinted. They waited with patience borne of years of waiting and standing in queues for nearly everything – for identity cards, for transport, for bail, for food and water, for housing, and for medical attention. Their training stood them in good stead on polling day. None walked away because the queues were too long. No one objected when they had to return the next day because the ballot boxes had been misrouted.

As I write the closing paragraphs of this narrative the most amazing election has taken place and opened South Africa up so that a democratic, multi-racial state may be created. When the ANC declared, on more than one occasion over the years, that what they were struggling for was a multi-racial state, not too many people outside their own ranks really believed them. Now it has happened it has amazed the world. The triumph of the people of South Africa led by Nelson Mandela and his colleagues is a lesson to the world that when the people fight together the impossible can be achieved. If the ANC with all their difficulties can lay the basis for a better life why cannot the people of Britain take advantage of all their wealth and also force a government which does not serve the people out of office?

Tiny Rowland

The smile on the face of capitalism

JOSEPH Conrad described one of his villains as a 'papier-mâché Mephistopheles'. That was always the public image of Tiny Rowland, who has died aged 80. His secretive nature and mocking smile seemed to fit perfectly with Edward Heath's descriptive tag — 'an unpleasant and unacceptable face of capitalism'.

When the basic facts about Tiny's background were eventually winnowed out, they all seemed of a piece. Despite his Old Etonian airs, he was born Roland Walter Fuhrhop and had been a *Scharführer* (troop-leader) in the Hitler Youth before his family moved to Britain in 1934. Although he adopted an English name, he was interned during the 1939-45 war under a regulation employed to round up fascists. When he emigrated after the war to what was Rhodesia, he began dealing in dodgy gold mines and later progressed to dispensing 'special payments' to sleazy presidents; they gave him rewarding contracts.

For all that, Tiny Rowland was a curiously vulnerable tycoon. His creation, the £2 billion Lonrho conglomerate, had been snatched from him in 1993 by Dieter Bock, an adroit German property developer brought in to resolve mounting debt problems. And there was Tiny's enduring bitterness that Mohamed al-Fayed had acquired Harrods, the prize Tiny most desired.

Tiny was litigious to extremes. He used lawyers like birdshot. His legal battles with al-Fayed, with major oil companies, with fellow-directors who had tried to oust him, with former partners in all cost Lonrho millions. There were endless boardroom battles. In the end, the 60,000 once-doting small shareholders could

ultimate goal — much of it made in Kenya. When need be he was ruthless: upon the death of Jomo Kenyatta, all relations of the newly-buried leader were sacked from their Lonrho posts, then Tiny turned his smile towards President Moi. Soon he gave him a fine stretch of farmland as the site for Moi University.

These instincts were inherited from his father, Hamburg-born Wilhelm Fuhrhop, who, in 1906 married, in what seems to have been a shotgun wedding, an Anglo-Dutch girl, Muriel Kauwenhoven. The Fuhrhop business flourished, but when the 1914-18 war began, the Fuhrhops were interned as aliens. In a well-guarded cantonment, east of Goa, Tiny was born and christened Roland Walter.

After the war the Fuhrhops made their way back from India to Hamburg, with two Indian servants — one of whom is reputed to have given Tiny — who would grow to over 6ft — his nickname. He went to Hamburg primary school, then entered the Heinrich-Hertz Gymnasium; there, like almost all his classmates, he enrolled in the Hitler Youth.

But in 1934, the family migrated to London. Mrs Fuhrhop was the driving force be-

From Rhodesia, Tiny saw newly-independent Africa up for grabs. He moved boldly in, treating the continent like one vast car-boot sale

changed his name to Rowland, and held a British passport because he was born in India, he could not disguise his origins. He became a private in the Royal Army Medical Corps. There was no risk of his meeting his brother on the battlefield!

Tiny spent three menial years in army hospitals in Scotland. His father was once again interned, this time in the Isle of Man, and Tiny Rowland was to join him, in the notorious Peel camp for high-risk Nazi sympathisers. Why this happened remains unclear. His wartime records are closely sealed. He always claimed that he went absent without leave, was arrested, sent back to Scotland, then taken under guard to Peel.

Some say he was committed to Peel for showing pro-Nazi sympathies, but there is no credible evidence of that. It is far more likely that he went there to become an informer, as the price of being near his mother, dying of cancer. Certainly he was suspected by fellow-detainees of being a spy.

Towards the end of the war he was transferred to the island's civilian camp and was with his mother when she died. Shortly after the war he lived in Mayfair, dealing in cars and importing oranges from Algeria.

Life took a decisive turn in 1948, when a business friend suggested that prospects looked splendid in what was then Rhodesia. It was an irresistible challenge: Tiny left Britain, taking his favourite Mercedes and leaving behind a large unpaid tax bill.

After 10 years of farming and dealing with mining prospects, Tiny was spotted by an aristocratic entrepreneur named Angus Ogilvy, who had interests in southern Africa. A new guiding hand was needed for Lonrho (the London and Rhodesia tradictory and enigmatic that many of those who tried to penetrate his facade imagined there must be a big secret within. In later years, it was generally accepted that he worked for British intelligence securing Britain's interests in post-colonial Africa. He also played a key role for Margaret Thatcher in putting together the Lancaster House conference which settled the future of Zimbabwe.

Tiny loved political intrigue, and tried to back winners in Africa. But often he got it wrong, bankrolling Joshua Nkomo in the belief that he would become Zimbabwe's president, and supporting the Unita leader Jonas Savimbi in Angola's civil war. At one moment Tiny would appear to be a lackey of the United States, at another he would praise Colonel Gaddafy declaring: "The Libyans are just retailers in terrorism, the Americans are wholesalers."

Money was always Tiny's and he was immediately made a corporal. A picture of the corps survives. Tiny stands out amid the rows of stolid faces because of his smile and the rakish angle of his peaked cap.

After leaving school at 18, he joined his father's import-export business in London, then joined the shipping company run by an uncle. Tiny's weekend enjoyment was driving fast cars around the Home Counties; he liked Mercedes. He also travelled in Europe, and liked boasting that he had been jailed by the Nazis for helping Jews smuggle out their possessions. It was an apocryphal tale. He loved weaving such fantasies about his background, including inventing relations.

In September 1939, Tiny's brother Raimund, doing his military service in Germany, joined the Wehrmacht, was commissioned, and fought all through the war. Military life was more humdrum for Tiny. Although he had hurriedly large question-mark over the background he had reluctantly disclosed to Ogilvy. A senior Lonrho director was Sir Joseph Ball, a former member of MI5 and deputy chairman of the secret spy-hunting Home Defence (Security) Executive during the second world war. If Sir Joseph raised no objection, Rowland must have been clean.

In 1961, Rowland was made joint managing director, alongside Sir Joseph's languid Old Etonian son, Alan. From the outset, there was no doubting who called the shots. Tiny looked north from Rhodesia, and saw newly-independent Africa up for grabs. He moved boldly in, treating the continent like one vast car-boot sale.

The results were slow at first, then spectacular. By 1973, Lonrho's pretax profits were hitting £20 million, by 1980, they were £120 million. Life on the personal front

Tiny Rowland . . . a vulnerable tycoon, and isolated after he lost control of Lonrho

PHOTOGRAPH: SEAN SMITH

was just as promising. The Honourable Angus had in 1963 become the husband of Princess Alexandra, the Queen's cousin. A few years later, Tiny gave up a longtime mistress and married Josephine Taylor, the daughter of a former business partner. She was less than half his age.

The Ogilvys and the Rowlands had adjoining flats in Park Lane. Often they met, in dressing-gowns, for leisurely breakfasts. Angus was on the Lonrho board, together with the Honourable Gerald Percy, all paying court to Tiny.

But the idyll did not last: in 1973, the great Lonrho boardroom battle erupted, over the mounting debts created by Rowland's more grandiose African schemes. It was the City sensation of the decade — and was to prompt Edward Heath's famous remark. Dirt was flung recklessly. When Angus deserted and resigned from the board, Tiny wrote to him furiously: "I will crucify you!" The rebels had wanted Gerald Percy as the new supremo, but Tiny won — with the backing of Lonrho's small shareholders.

For Tiny the affair seemed like a stupendous victory, but he was now branded as an outsider and no longer welcome in the better sort of boardroom. He grew paranoid, surrounded himself with sycophants, travelled compulsively round Africa, showed signs of megalomania, and launched interminable lawsuits. The profits kept rising for some years, but so did the debts. The old magic had gone. "I have no friends," he said aggressively.

There was solace in family life, with Josie and their four children. They had a mansion beside the Thames in Buckinghamshire, a house in Chester Square, an apartment in Mexico, a yacht in the Mediterranean and use of the Lonrho jet.

One venture of Rowland's later years was the purchase of the Observer, in 1981. He was greeted with an hostility close to loathing, was allowed to interfere editorially, and left the paper — it was sold to the Guardian group in 1993 — even weaker than when he had acquired it. As part of his extraordinary feud with al-Fayed, Tiny had forced Mrs Thatcher to launch an investigation into al-Fayed's takeover of Harrods. When the Department of Trade and Industry refused to publish it, Tiny did so, in a special weekday edition of the Observer.

Losing Harrods had been the bitterest blow. He wanted to own the store. The al-Fayeds had outsmarted him by using the House of Fraser shares he had sold to them for more than £100 million — temporarily, as he thought, to improve just one year's Lonrho balance sheet. He never got over it.

The ferocious diatribes he published were brilliant, but could not save the day. Although his invective made adversaries cringe, Tiny Rowland was too headstrong, his behaviour too impetuous for him ever to have stayed the course as a giant of capitalism. He was a unique opportunist, whose charisma faded with the years.

Richard Hall

Roland "Tiny" Walter Rowland (Fuhrhop), businessman, born November 27, 1917; died July 24, 1998

Letters

Richard Fox writes: It's a pity that your sympathetic obituary of Kenneth Barnes *(June 22)* omitted his key role in the group of 11 Friends whose *Towards a Quaker View of Sex* (1963, revised 1964 and reprinted at least four times) played such a large part in changing attitudes towards sexuality, especially homosexuals, who were still being hounded by police.

However, when, some years ago, the York Meeting (of which he was an elder) was being asked to recognise a "marriage" between two gay members, he and I agreed that our group never envisaged things moving that far.

When Frances died after a long and debilitating illness he married Eleanor, an ex-pupil who became director of the family fund of the Joseph Rowntree Foundation. He rejoiced in her work as he did in her Roman Catholicism.

Too bad that your photo of him looks more like Michael Foot than the KCB I knew and loved.

Ann V. Read writes: In your obituary *(June 13)* of Johnny Johnston, you stated that the words of the first sung commercial at the launch of ITV in 1955 were written by Harold Barnes. However, credit for composing the jingle "Murray-mints, Murray-mints, the too-good-to-hurry mints" rests with my late father Stanley Penn, a copywriter at S H Bensons.

Nan Berger

Communism's warm heart

NAN Berger, who has died aged 84, was awarded an OBE in the New Year's honours of 1948. Nothing odd in that, of course. Except that Nan was 33 at the time, a committed (though by that time probably not card-carrying) communist and a fairly lowly civil servant in the statistical department of the Ministry of Fuel and Power.

In the appalling deep-frozen winter of 1947, Nan was picked out by under-secretary Francis Hemming to work with him on getting such fuel as there was fairly and rationally distributed. This appealed to Nan's socialism and her organising abilities. All protocol discarded, she toured the country to find out what was really happening. With no statistical qualifications, she devised with Hemming a "numerate presentation" on which government plans to meet the fuel crisis were based.

Nan Berger was born near Manchester. Her father was a prosperous industrialist; the family home was comfortable but without any intellectual stimulation. So in 1935, Nan escaped to London, ostensibly to look after her brother, Peter, who was studying at the London School of Economics. And they both joined the Communist Party.

Nan Berger . . . an unorthodox civil servant

She struggled to read, and subsequently accepted, Marxism, but she was essentially a doer, not a theoretician. She had a passionate concern for the individual. Typical of this was the way that, on joining the Bank of England in 1940 (her first real job), she set about establishing a staff committee to represent the temporary clerks. She was summarily dismissed soon after, when the Bank looked into her political background. (The Bank apparently did not divulge its information since Nan was immediately taken on by the Civil Service.) Nan left the Civil Service to bring up her children and she spent much of the rest of her life as a freelance journalist.

For many years, she edited Hospitality, the journal for the Hotel and Catering International Management Association. This led her into an interest in school meals, which she maintained had an educational and social purpose, not just a nutritional one. She later wrote a book on the subject.

The position of women attracted her interest during the war when she saw temporary clerks (all women, of course) exploited and patronised, and again, after the war, when they were sent back to the home again. She was the co-author of *Woman — Fancy or Free*, a lively, early discussion on the status of women, published in 1962. Similarly, she helped pioneer discussion on children's rights, and, in 1973, wrote a Penguin handbook on the subject.

Nan travelled widely — to learn first-hand about political movements. In 1939, she got to North America to attend the Congress of the League of American Writers, and to study the impact of President Roosevelt's New Deal policies.

Much later she went to South Africa. In 1962, Helen Joseph, newly released from five years under house arrest, arranged for Nan to join her on a trip to make contact with various units of the Federation of South African Women and to look for "banished" people. They visited townships and state farms where whites were forbidden.

In her seventies, she became a governor of her local school in Islington, north London, and was taken on to help slow readers. A spell in a recuperative hospital in her eighties led to her being asked to run a discussion group there for patients.

Nan never lost her basic faith in Marxism and all her life battled her enemy, capitalism. Nan possessed a supreme talent for friendship. She was devoted and loyal. No life could have been richer or more fulfilled on a personal level, and no one filled the unforgiving minute as well as she did.

She was married to Roland Berger and they had two daughters.

Susan Marsden

Nan (Nancie) Elizabeth Berger, journalist, political activist, born March 8, 1914; July 16, 1998

A Country Diary

NORTHUMBERLAND: Steely grey skies, not conducive to picking soft fruit, sent me instead into the woods. Not ideal weather conditions for watching wildlife either, but I know where to look.

Midsummer brings midges and tall undergrowth, but at dawn beasts emerge to socialise and browse. Ten years ago, British Coal disrupted plantations with opencast mining on our north-east coast, excavating seams up to the fringes of some places, so that they became untenable to bird or beast. Now, with great sensitivity, the land has been restored, hedgerows planted, copses laid down and wetland sites for wildfowl created. One birch plantation has been untenable for years; I have despaired that it would ever come to life again. This spring the bluebells came out, the smell of garlic pervaded the air again, self-seeded brambles, willow-herb and grasses have revived. Rowan trees and wild rose bushes are colouring, stoats, rabbits and mice rustle in fallen leaves and chaffinches, their wings splashed with yellow, are packing in twittering flocks.

The lost wood is coming to life again. I have not seen the yellow vixen there yet, she has found a quiet place to live, but I have seen her in the sand dunes, picking her way through the marram grass, snuffling at rabbit burrows. She may return. Last night a fine roe buck emerged from some larches less than 50 yards from where I stood.

Accompanying him was a yearling buck, the young beast acting as consort and watcher for the elder, a mutually beneficial arrangement seen between males of all deer species. They look in good condition. Perhaps, in the long term, the deer may benefit from the enforced absence because, having travelled, they will have interbred with other deer colonies in the neighbourhood.

VERONICA HEATH

Birthdays

Michael Ball, singer, 36; **Allan Border**, cricketer, 43; **Roseanna Cunningham**, Scot Nat MP, 47; **Christopher Dean**, ice skater, 40; **Jo Durie**, tennis player, 38; **Bobbie Gentry**, singer, 56; **Gabrielle Glaister**, actress, 38; **Elizabeth Hardwick**, writer, 82; **Jack Higgins** (Harry Patterson), novelist, 69; **Lord Jenkins of Putney**, former Labour minister, 90; **Ernie Ross**, Labour MP, 56; **Joy Whitby**, pioneer of children's television, 68; **Baroness (Shirley) Williams**, Liberal Democrat peer, 68.

Image Credits

Acknowledgements

We would like to thank Vicki Berger for all her generous help and commitment to making this publication possible, and allowing us to access her family archives. The Freedom Festival Arts Trust, in particular Mikey Martins and Lindsay Stockley for inviting us to commission this book with Ruth Ewan as part of Beyond Words, Hull, and James Reckitt Library Trust for supporting the work.

Also for all their help and support in realising this project: Liberty Archives and Simon Wilson at Hull History Centre; Anna Towlson, Archives and Special Collections Manager, LSE Library; Hugh Alexander, National Archives Image Library Deputy Manager; Nick Evans and Beki Bloomfield at WISE; Mike Hill, Hull Central Library; Meirian Jump and Rose Brown at the Marx Memorial Library and Worker's School; Dawn Power at the Morning Star; Stuart at Idea Digital; Kevin Buyers, Richard Baxell, Emma Ewan, Jenny Fisher, Alison Light, Sheila Rowbotham, Jill Shaw, and Joseph Whittaker.

Colophon

Twenty-Nine Thousand Nights

A Communist Life
Nan Berger

A project by Ruth Ewan
Published and distributed by
Book Works

Edited by Ruth Ewan
and Gavin Everall
**Transcription of original
autobiography** Deborah Lim
Photography by Nicole Bachmann
Proofreading Jenny Fisher
Designed by osasto.net

Cover image Nan Berger,
Vicki Berger family archive

Epilogue text featured on a fruit and
veg stall, Covent Garden, featured in
the article on unionisation of market
porters, by Nan Berger, *Holborn
Outlook*, 1938

Typeset in Concorde,
Bureau Grotesque

Printed by Tallinn Book Printers

Published by Book Works as part
of *Beyond Words* with the Freedom
Festival Arts Trust, Hull Culture and
Leisure Library Services and Book
Works, in association with Hull
History Centre, Wilberforce Institute
for the study of Slavery and
Emancipation, University of Hull,
funded by James Reckitt Library
Trust and Arts Council England.

Book Works receives
National Portfolio funding from
Arts Council England.

ISBN 978 1 906012 86 1

Book Works, 19 Holywell Row,
London EC2A 4JB

www.bookworks.org.uk
telephone: +44 (0)207 247 2203

THE FRUITS OF THE EARTH CAN BE YOURS